One Voice Rising

Sagebrush near Clifford Duncan's childhood home in Whiterocks, Utah.

APRIL 15, 1991

One Voice Rising

The Life of Clifford Duncan

CLIFFORD DUNCAN

with LINDA SILLITOE

PHOTOGRAPHS BY *George R. Janecek*

FOREWORD BY *Forrest Cuch*

THE UNIVERSITY OF UTAH PRESS
Salt Lake City

The Defiance House Man colophon is a registered trademark of The University
of Utah Press. It is based on a four-foot-tall Ancient Puebloan pictograph (late PIII)
near Glen Canyon, Utah.

LIBRARY OF CONGRESS CATALOGING-IN-PUBLICATION DATA

Names: Duncan, Clifford, author. | Sillitoe, Linda, 1948-2010, transcriber. | Janecek,
George R. (George Rudolf), 1946- photographer (expression) Title: One voice rising : the
life of Clifford Duncan / Clifford Duncan and Linda Sillitoe ; photographs by George R.
Janecek. Description: Salt Lake City : University of Utah Press, [2019] | Identifiers: LCCN
2018048122 (print) | LCCN 2018050697 (ebook) | ISBN 9781607816874 (ebook) | ISBN
9781607817031 (paper) | ISBN 9781607816867 (cloth : alk. paper) Subjects: LCSH: Duncan,
Clifford. | Indian healers--Biography. | Ute Indians--Biography. | Ute Indians--History. |
Native American Church of North America. | Ute Indians--Religion. | Indians of North
America--Poetry. Classification: LCC E99.U8 (ebook) | LCC E99.U8 D79 2019 (print) | DDC
979.004/9745760092 [B] —dc23 LC record available at https://lccn.loc.gov/2018048122

Errata and further information on this and other titles available online at UofUpress.com

Printed and bound in the United States of America.

Earth Teach Me

There is a road in the hearts of all of us, hidden and seldom traveled,
which leads to an unknown, secret place.
The old people came literally to love the soil,
and they sat or reclined on the ground with a feeling of
being close to a mothering power.
Their teepees were built upon the earth
and their altars were made of earth.
The soul was soothing, strengthening, cleansing and healing.
That is why the old Indian still sits upon the earth instead of
propping himself up and away from its life giving forces.
For him, to sit or lie upon the ground is to be able to think more deeply
and to feel more keenly. He can see more clearly into the mysteries of
life and come closer in kinship to other lives about him.

—Chief Luther Standing Bear

Contents

Foreword

Forrest Cuch, *March 2017*

The Ute Indian Tribe of the Uintah and Ouray Reservation has had many great people, inspiring leaders, and powerful medicine people. Clifford Duncan was one of them, as was his great-grandfather John. Clifford was born and raised on the Ute Reservation located in northeastern Utah. He was a participant in the historic pattern of mid-twentieth century reservation life in the area referred to as the Uinta Basin. First came his strong traditional upbringing in a Ute family living in the northern portion of the reservation, near the base of the Uinta Mountains. They had a rural livelihood, filled with riding horses, long stays with relatives, and learning Ute ways. Then came exile in the federal boarding school system, followed by the many turns of young adulthood, city living, and eventually a return home. As the old people say, "We all return home sooner or later."

With adulthood had come marriage and a brief urban lifestyle. He was a trendsetter as an early stay-at-home dad when his wife was working in the medical field in Salt Lake City, Utah. His life would take many turns. He returned home to the reservation and served in numerous roles in tribal government, from tribal councilman on the governing Ute Business Committee to museum curator; all the while serving as Native American Church spiritual leader (Roadman) to the Utes and eventually ambassador to many members of the religion in Utah and the surrounding area. Although he was cautious of the challenges that face spiritual leaders who are active in secular activities and governance, he became a long-time spokesman for Indian people, especially but not only in Utah.

What I remember most about Clifford Duncan is how he carried himself. He always presented himself well, with straight stature, clean looks, and well-focused determination. He dressed well, always neat in appearance and appointment. He had very fine features that amplified his good looks and slim physique. These features would serve him well during the latter part of his life and culminate in his many leadership roles, including as the colorful, staff-bearing Ute tribal representative in the Opening Ceremony of the 2002 Winter Olympic Games.

Clifford was an outstanding artist. His work was diagrammatic and pictorial before such graphic art achieved its current popularity. He designed the cover of several Ute Indian books that grace our libraries and archives.

Linda Sillitoe, perhaps to an unknowing extent, reveals the many sides to Clifford. He could be very stoic at times, to use an old adjective that is overused to describe Indians. And yet Clifford could also be fun and jovial, and most of all, he was always devoted to his relatives. The love and patience he bestowed upon his young family was precious.

Clifford was highly respected for his strong spiritual beliefs. In one story I heard this narrative: A lady said a few days before Clifford was to arrive at their ranch in Colorado, the strangest thing occurred. A herd of about three elk arrived in their back yard, and they stayed there during Clifford's entire visit. She asked him about them and he calmly replied, "Oh, they are my helpers."

"This was a common occurrence in the life of Clifford Duncan.

Clifford was a complex man and he made mistakes in his life as we all do, but what is special about this book is that it gives a glimpse of how he, as a Ute man, transcended and moved forward in his life to make many contributions. This is what is so important for young people to see and understand. His life was an excellent example of human adaptation to cultural change.

One of the things that is revealed in the book is how much Clifford was a thinking man. He was always contemplating and wondering about different things and experiences. He liked to discuss things as they occurred to him, often laughing at his thoughts and interpretations. Clifford was fun to be around, and yet, he could become dead serious at times.

He held an eclectic view of religion and was open to many different traditions and beliefs. He was staunchly protective of and stubborn to retain those beliefs he held dear. On the other hand, he was always open to learning new viewpoints about spiritual ideas and religious systems. During the latter part of his life, Clifford devoted time and energy to St. Paul's Episcopal Church in Whiterocks, Utah. He was a close friend of Reverend Sue Duffield and her husband, Jim. He donated a huge tipi to the church, which he often volunteered to set up for various uses. Clifford readily offered his sweat lodge to practitioners who were interested in supplementing their spiritual development with other kinds of services.

And he continued to make himself available to his tribe and people upon call. He was always ready to conduct a ceremony or a peyote meeting or available and willing to preside over a death in a family or other important event in the lives of his people. He was an important person in the lives of the Ute people and other native people of the surrounding western region. He is greatly missed and will continue to be remembered for many years to come.

Preface

Carolyn Janecek

Clifford Duncan, Linda Sillitoe, and George Janecek began working on *One Voice Rising* before I was born, but I grew up familiar with my dad's documentary photography and his collaboration with the University of Utah to preserve people's histories. After moving to Utah myself, I was finally able to meet Clifford Duncan in person, after having seen his life in photos and reading Sillitoe's manuscript. Clifford had been invited to carry the flame at the 2002 Olympic Winter Games and years had passed since the original completion of the memoir. Because there was a gap in his story, several years after Linda Sillitoe's death I volunteered to interview Clifford in his home during the summer of 2013. The final two chapters of this book are the result of those interviews.

Clifford was almost entirely blind by then and as we spoke he told me how he could still remember the local landmarks and be his daughter's navigator in the car—despite not being able to see the road. He had a great sense of humor, especially as he recalled the Olympic ceremonies and the jokes he played then. Even as he joked around and shared old memories from his worn recliner, he reflected on the separation between the United States and Native Americans; he understood that although people, culture, and legislation may have changed, the original distinction between *us* and *them* has remained, present over centuries of forced assimilation.

Even so, Clifford remained hopeful about preserving Ute culture as he recalled how his son asked him about Ute words and put them into his songs. Clifford saw how languages and traditions adapt over time and recognized that change can be okay, as long as young people want to reconnect with their culture and take care of their traditions for the generations to come.

As I was transcribing his interviews, I wanted to stay as true to Clifford's words as Linda Sillitoe did. This memoir is a part of the history Clifford wanted to preserve with all his memories, hope, and the words, "I'll be all right."

Introduction

Linda Sillitoe, *October 1992*

How does one introduce Clifford Duncan—a man who asks for "unleaded" sugar in his coffee, yet if he should get a headache in the forest, will chew on bark for aspirin-like relief?

During the last decade, the name Clifford Duncan has appeared fairly frequently in northern Utah media, variously identified as museum curator for the Ute Tribe, a Ute tribal councilman, a medicine man, a spiritual leader, and the president of the Native American Church of Utah. No title in English describes him precisely within the Indian realm where his knowledge of worlds past and present and his strength of spirit are often in demand.

Clifford is simultaneously one of the most bicultural and traditional American Indians in the West, possibly in the nation. Both aspects keep him on the move, between the forests and ruins of the Uintah-Ouray Reservation in eastern Utah and various big cities, towns, and numerous Indian reservations. His position as tribal councilman sends him to Washington, DC, to Phoenix, Arizona, and elsewhere for conferences and meetings. He visits Salt Lake City to testify before legislative committees, to counsel government officials, to consult with museum and historical bodies, to "talk fast" with the attorney friend who gives him the first hour of consultation free, to spiritually cleanse a clinic where a baby spontaneously aborted, to participate in seminars and on programs, and to minister spiritually to friends.

As a leader in the Native American Church, he travels widely to conduct all-night meetings and healing ceremonies. Other regional meetings are political, convened to develop strategies to protect the freedom to practice native religions.

Before his election to the governing Ute Tribal Council (also called the Business Committee) in 1991, his skills as a certified paralegal and a certified archeologist supported his position as curator of the Ute Tribal Museum. Frequently, energy companies, archeologists, and developers still require his services when they encounter burials and other traditional sites on reservation lands. Even as an archeologist and museum director, Clifford honors the burials, leaving the dead and their possessions at rest whenever possible. In case of a conflict, his spiritual beliefs take priority.

Near midnight, at the annual Fort Duchesne powwow in 1991, after most non-Indians had left, Clifford presided over a memorial giveaway for an elderly couple who had died several years earlier. He described them as "one of the last couples who did spiritual doctoring." Following the honor song, the grandson sponsoring the ceremony told the crowd he was presenting the beautiful white tepee, looming above the announcer's stand, to Clifford, in memory of his grandparents and in order to perpetuate native ceremony. Clifford accepted the tepee, promising it would be used only for that purpose.

Well into the process of writing this book together, Clifford and I tried to reconstruct how this rather unlikely work began. As a journalist, I had crossed enough boundaries socially, culturally, mentally, and emotionally that I did not fully comprehend the barriers my being Anglo, from a Mormon background, and female presented—in that order. The events that brought us together are easier to recall than the invisible bridges we must have erected bit by bit, which became apparent only after we had crossed them.

As a newspaper writer, in the early 1980s, I began covering Native American issues in Utah—hardly a mandatory beat. As I researched the Ute tribe and visited the Uintah-Ouray Reservation, I was repeatedly advised, "You really ought to talk to Clifford Duncan." He knew about tribal history, about native religion, about jurisdiction and Indian law from a Ute viewpoint. I gathered that he was respected and somewhat controversial among scholars and among the Utes. I intuited that he was a reserved man who would not seek and might discourage publicity.

Clifford doesn't remember how we met, but I do. Returning from a family vacation late one summer, we entered the museum en masse and I introduced myself to Clifford, who was polite but taciturn. Several weeks later I called, inquiring about the old photographs he had in the museum, and we began to become acquainted. Occasionally Clifford would call me at the newspaper and announce, "The Indian is coming to the big city," and we would meet at a nearby mall to chat over coffee, soft drinks, or breakfast. They were intense chats, once I drew him out. His depth, his cynicism, and his authenticity challenged me. Eventually, I convinced him to let me write a profile of him for the Sunday magazine by focusing it on what "Indian-ness" means.

He never gave me a resume, but through visiting his home and spending time with him, I learned that he was an artist whose paintings had been both exhibited and sold. He was a trained lay archeologist whose fascination with the subject only complemented his strong spiritual views. He conducted religious meetings in the tepee in his backyard. He was a horseman, a hunter, a husband, father, and grandfather.

The profile I wrote was as in-depth as could fit in the magazine, but I sensed that Clifford felt it was superficial. Ironically, I also knew that for him, as for most Indian people I wrote about, being singled out had its discomforts. Nevertheless, when I proposed three Native American books to the University of Utah Press, one was—unbeknownst to him—a biography of Clifford Duncan.

However, in 1986, my newspaper career and coverage of minority issues was interrupted by a decision to write a book on a complicated tragedy in my own culture involving forgeries and bombings in Salt

Lake City. Amid the general fascination around this living murder mystery, only my Indian friends could not understand why I was taking on such a bizarre project. I learned to say, "This happened on my turf; this is my tribe. I have to do this."

During the next two years when I was consumed and eventually drained by that book, I heard from Clifford now and then. In early 1988 I found myself unchained from the computer and looking for sunlight. I pulled out the proposal to the University of Utah Press and wrote to Clifford, suggesting that together we write his biography. In the over-lunch conversation that followed, the barriers and distances between us were clear, yet he agreed as I felt he would.

Soon afterward George Janecek, whose remarkable photographs I knew particularly from *The Other Utahns*, called and suggested working together on Indian projects. He, too, knew Clifford and became excited about the prospect of a book. Clifford and I began our talks and I began writing. Late in 1989, we all signed a contract with the press and our work began in earnest.

By that time, intercultural politics had shifted. The United States Supreme Court had upheld the original boundaries of the Uintah-Ouray Reservation, meaning non-Indian towns such as Duchesne and Roosevelt came under Ute jurisdiction. Always touchy, many issues in the border towns became inflamed. Even more important to our work was the Supreme Court ruling that off-reservation peyote meetings and non-Indians using peyote are not protected by the freedom of religion. This made the presence of non-Indians at ceremonies extremely sensitive. George Janecek already could not photograph sweat lodge ceremonies or the Sun Dance. Now peyote meetings, adapted toward healing or giving thanks, were also out of bounds— not only for the camera but for us. Although we both would continue to observe Clifford within his community, most of our work together required a separate setting.

Geographically, Clifford and I met either on the reservation or in the city or, preferably, in transit, taping our talks in his pickup truck or my car. Yet we met more essentially on turf we created ourselves, between cultures. We noticed our differences most when we came in contact with other people—Indian or non-Indian. Suddenly, we were contained again by our skin colors, our genders, our cultures. The curiosity or distaste we felt from others was a subtle but persistent reminder we live in different worlds.

We enjoyed the cultural ironies. Once Clifford and I drove away from my suburban home during rush hour—not of traffic but of joggers, walkers and bikers, exercising away the results of a too-opulent lifestyle. "Where are all these people going?" Clifford asked humorously. "It looks like a parade. Maybe everyone's going to see an accident or something."

I chuckled. "Don't people jog or walk in Neola?"

He considered. "No. It used to be that way. Indian people would walk into town, walk to the store. Then we got automobiles."

Like many Native Americans who live on or near reservations, Clifford spends a good deal of his time in his pickup truck. The radar sensor on the dashboard, the arrowhead and medallions hanging from the rearview mirror, the gallon jug of water on the cab floor, the denim jacket on the seat beside him, and—sometimes—the box of healing instruments under the jacket bespeak a variety and efficiency that is remarkable. Once when Clifford visited me in Salt Lake City, he asked for newspaper and tape or string before leaving. He had stopped to cut sage along Highway 40 through the mountains. In a few minutes, he left with an artistically contrived package encompassing the aromatic sage.

One bright winter morning as we drove west toward Vernal, Clifford slid a tape into the tape deck in his truck and adjusted the volume. "Here are some great Indian classics," he announced. The strains of "Glow Little Glow Worm," popular during his teenage years, filled the cab.

Other times our cultural differences surfaced in odd if trivial ways. Approaching a café for lunch, for instance, we reached the door at the same time. By the old rules of my society (which Clifford, of course, knows), he would open the door and hold it open for me to enter first. By the old rules of his society (which he has explained to me), he would open the door and enter first with me following. By my rules and those of my contemporaries, whoever reaches the door first opens it and then after a moment of casual confusion someone goes in first, following a subliminal signal of convenience or deference. So how did we get through the doors? We were too engrossed in our thoughts or in conversation to notice, but we found ourselves inside, ordering lunch.

Although Clifford left the logistics of publishing to me, he was very conscious of the product. "This is not," he said once, "another *Black Elk Speaks*." Native religion is the core of his life. He saw it as the necessary core of this book despite the secrecy he and other native people employ to protect its continuity. However, he did not want to give the impression in the least degree that he considers himself a spokesman for the Utes, for Native Americans, for the Native American Church, or for healers and shamans, or that his ways are right or true for everyone. We agreed this work would represent itself as an individual life and viewpoint, an ethnobiography including a bicultural discussion of current issues.

He was conscious, too, of style as his words returned to him in draft form. Our methodology was verbal, fitting his natural eloquence and the oral tradition of his people, and also my long experience in interviewing. Spoken language differs from written language, tending to be more casual, more colloquial, more digressive. Gestures and other visual cues don't transfer into print. However, since most of Clifford's discourse was very focused, long passages were adopted into the text virtually verbatim. Our discussions ranged widely and sometimes circled back, adding detail or enhancing perspective. When I transcribed the tapes and wove the conversation into the manuscript, I adjusted and clarified syntax as necessary. He did the same as he read and annotated the drafts.

"You read a lot of books of Indian poetry," Clifford commented one day as he returned several lightly marked chapters and prepared for another taping session, this one in Roosevelt. "Who made that poetry? Was it the Indian?—or was it just a saying he came up with? You read quotations made by—for instance—Sitting Bull. It sounds so pretty. Maybe he didn't really talk like that. Some writer wrote it that way and passed it on, and eventually it became the way we read it. You find a difference between the way an Indian talks and the way English is spoken."

I agreed, but with reservations. From my earliest discussions with Clifford, I was aware that he often spoke a spontaneous poetry. Once I had captured his narrative voice on tape, I had indulged my curiosity to see if some of his oratory would scan poetically. What follows is his answer to my question later that same day: "Why are you writing this book? Who is your real audience?" He said:

> I think about different things
> going through my everyday life,
> going to ceremonies,
> talking to people.
> You try to get people together
> to talk with them.
> You find that certain people will listen;
> different groups will listen too.
> Yet the one you're always trying to reach,
> you can't seem to reach.
> One day, he or she may want to listen,
> but you're not there.
> If someday they want to listen,
> they can read my book and say,
> "This is what he said."
> I guess it's my own people
> I'm talking to, in a way,

> I think my people will understand
> me better in a book.
> They will understand what I say.
> Writing a book is somewhat a delayed message.
> Then, too, they can pick up
> From the things I have learned,
> fill in the gaps,
> and take it from there.
> They can have a better life."

Registering his complaint about "poetizing" Indian voices, I struggled to express how I think poetry happens. However, Clifford was ahead of me as he concluded, "I think what it comes down to is that the writer is trying to capture the spiritual meaning in the writing. I think that's where the change takes place." Yes—but poetry can be inherent in the speech, as well.

He then illuminated our talks in a way that reflects significant cultural implications for both our peoples, past and present.

"In a language such as Ute, the language is merely a supplement to how I feel or how I would like to see certain things happen," he said. "I assume that you already know what I'm going to say; then a word will add to that or open the door. But when we talk, we are actually guiding the person by the way we feel. This communication is a spiritual communication. A spiritual communication could be what I'm telling to you, but I will say a few words here and there. I'm leading you with these words; in the same way, you would lead me."

For someone for whom words are process and product, this manipulable clay from which text can be molded, this intuitive approach was disorienting. "I assume that you already know what I am going to say" was an astonishing statement considering the borders we crossed and the complexity of the culture and metaphysics I was trying to comprehend. Yet as Clifford talked, I did understand in ways I could not articulate or always recall when I replayed his words on tape. The flow of communication was swifter and deeper than the stepping-stone words. That much was familiar from other intense interviews. What differed with Clifford was that the entire flow was known and acknowledged—said or unsaid, it counted.

As a writer, I relied on language as inevitably revealing of its speaker, yet I routinely supplemented my interviews by noting body language, clothing, office decor, or home furnishings to give the reader added insight. I had learned to pay attention to my own reactions during an interview. Rapport, the pale professional word for the spiritual communication Clifford described, is essential.

However, by the unspoken rules of the dominant society, feelings and intentions on both sides do not count if they are unexpressed. Interviewer and interviewee can lay some cards on the table and withhold others; the focus is on conversation and on behavior. Any speculation on the other person's subtext is guarded by the rational mind, which suggests bias, emotionalism, or paranoia as prompting our reactions. Usually I could assume that the interviewee was less observant than me, preoccupied with expressing his or her thoughts, and concerned only that I quote words and meaning accurately—challenge enough.

On a deeper level, I realized that in my verbal culture, silence is its own communicator and censor, hushing everything that does not fall harmoniously upon all ears. Silence sets the boundaries of thought and behavior, curbing the irreverent, inappropriate, vulgar, or even the controversial. At the same time, silence is a shield. One is not accountable for the thoughts seething in silence; one cannot be reproved for the unexpressed opinion.

Silence plays a different role in Clifford's less verbal, intuitive culture. What is felt is known and carries responsibility. Therefore speech, when needed, is given more weight. "If I do that he is going to say something about it," means a reprimand is coming, which is taken as such. "I have to talk to those people," does not describe a casual or civil encounter. It means spiritual counseling, in the context of family. Words are recognized as implements, knives or bandages. Only echoes in English remind those of us who are inundated by advertising, propaganda, and mass communication that in common parlance we give a "talking to," "put in our two bits," or ask, "Can we talk?" with emphasis beyond the literal. We even give "looks that could kill."

Using words to open doors, Clifford explained, "you are actually guiding the person by the way you feel." The implications of that statement strike deeper than the popular awareness of "picking up vibes" or "psyching out" friends, foes, employees, or employers. It suggests that all we think, speak, and analyze is controlled by a deeper dialogue of feeling, memory, and awareness that most of us ignore. I began to wonder if, for five hundred years, people within minority cultures simply had read the subtext of white America's discourse, accounting for much mistrust. Perhaps the "white man's" overtures were met in literally irrational but very logical ways.

Probably the most important shift in my relationship with Clifford occurred unintentionally. Soon after my true crime book was published, I began to experience odd events that I could not explain or dismiss, incidents I called "weird" and my expert friends in psychology called "paranormal." Incredulously, I learned that I have delved so deeply into my own cultural heart of darkness that I could not disengage. When several educated experts suggested methods learned from shamanism, or said, "This is when you call a medicine man," I thought how lucky I was to know one. When the chance came, I asked Clifford—little knowing what I was asking—if I could confide in him.

My circuitous and bizarre account seemed to open like a map for him, although he still found it hard to understand why I'd ever written that book. He agreed to help me if I could accept his ways. Only later did I realize that in requesting and accepting his help, I became the subject and he the expert on his own essential turf. Within that context, I experienced ceremony—and power—that would have been difficult for me to observe otherwise. Gradually I realized that the open mind I maintained regarding things mystical was literally a blind through which I could never comprehend the spiritual world Clifford moves in.

I began this project, I admit, hoping to preserve a vanishing viewpoint; to a degree, Clifford shares that idea. Now I share his view that Indian religion is becoming strong as American materialism wakens and as technology grows ever more deadly. Our opposite cultures, each caged, seem to hold one another's keys: education and employment versus the power of mind and spirit.

Native Americans see themselves as not only conquered but cheated, and history bears them out. Clifford adds that no gift can be received unless it is given, not stolen. "Americans own this land in the physical sense, but in the spiritual sense, the country still belongs to Native Americans because we never gave it away."

I reflect on five hundred years of violence to people in this hemisphere, to land and water, to wildlife, to culture, to language, and I understand the legacy of violence in our cities and families. I think how much healing must be done within and between cultures, and overwhelmed, remember what I tell my writing students: Begin anywhere; begin where you are.

Here is my teacher and friend, Clifford Duncan, wearer of many hats. In my mind's eye, he wears his black reservation hat and drives his truck. His song rises, the heel of one hand beating the steering wheel, his chant as singular and authentic as the land he travels. An eagle hovers over the cliff, and the road opens before him.

1

Indian Healing Ways

One evening, quite late at night, the telephone rang at my home. One of the younger members of the Ridley family asked for me, Clifford Duncan. The call concerned a young man who was in the hospital in Roosevelt, about fifteen miles from my home. I was told that the doctors couldn't find anything wrong with him, but he was experiencing pain in his chest. The family thought maybe I could help.

I drove down to the hospital and spoke to the young man, who was waiting for me there in a hospital bed. "What's wrong with you?" I asked him.

"I tried to tell the doctor but he won't listen," he replied. "A few days ago some spirit people came into my house through the front door. One of them shot me in the heart with a spirit arrow. I have to have that taken out."

My fingers probed the place in his ribs that he showed me. I could feel something in there.

"I don't know a lot about this kind of thing," I told him, "but I do know a little. I'll try to help you."

I did what I could, a version of the shamanic work done within the Sun Dance, and the young man thanked me. Soon he felt better, and he left the hospital.

For a long time I have been involved with Indian healing ways. I do not look at my religion as being old or pagan; it's not like that. It is something I use to talk about life today, not yesterday. Hopefully we will not lose our religion, our culture, the things we were taught.

Hopefully we will use our religion with the idea that it has advanced and can be used like anything else on this world.

I have been called a medicine man or a spiritual leader. I don't know how to define that term, as used by non-Indians. A *puwaghat* in our language is almost like a Christ. A *puwaghat* possesses certain powers, can make a person invisible, or make a river run backward, or make it rain when the land is dry. When a big cloud is coming, he can split that in half, saying, "Okay, you go this way," like Moses, in the *Old Testament*—he did that. He was a *puwaghat*. To Indians trying to interpret the word into English, Moses or Christ would be a medicine man or a spiritual leader. So when you have this other healer over here, helping people, the whites will call him a medicine man. Then Indians will say, "Well, he's not a medicine man," and they are right, too, because they know this person does not possess those powers.

I am a believer in Indian medicine ways. I do not perform miracles. I cannot make people disappear. I cannot make a rain stop. But I will take the position of asking God to help me stop the rain, and I'll tell him why. If a person comes to me and says, "I'm sick. I want you to help me," I will say okay. I am going to talk to him through a ritual that is set up in a certain way. That's the only thing I can do. His condition may change, or I'll give him the reason why it won't change.

Praying is talking to people and talking to God; talking to people through their spirit, to him who is inside of them, to the Man That Made This World. People have healing powers within themselves. All people have the power within to make themselves well. If you go to somebody and say, "Help me," this person merely pulls the power out of you so you can heal yourself. They bring it out by talking to the spirit that controls you. You're the one that made yourself well.

People cannot be treated all the same way; treatment must be individualized. A while ago my wife said to me, "I think I have an ulcer. My stomach hurts."

I said to her, "Go see the doctor." She did and he gave her a prescription for medicine that helped her. A little later an older Indian woman came to me with the same symptoms. I said, "Here is an herbal tea that will help you get well." She drank the tea and soon was well again.

She understood medicine ways the same way I do; a lot of this depends on how you were brought up.

The place where I grew up, east of Whiterocks, is overgrown now. Every so many years I go back to that place by myself, but then I say this: "Let the boy that was me and the boys who were my brothers come out. I know you're still here. I want you to listen to me. I'm a man now, traveling an amazing road that some may want to follow. I want you to help me, grown up now and getting old."

The ceremony I hold on to now is no stranger to me or to my brothers. *Puwa*—spirit—is personal. There is no ready word for ceremony, tradition, the Indian way, a part of life. Everything was Indian then, when I was a boy. They had to explain to us about the white man's side. Now everything is in the white man's world and we teach Indian ways.

The Ute language is important because you think the way you speak. When you go to an Indian ceremony, at first they will begin in English especially if it is a mixed group. But when they get down to where they are really sincere, down to the bottom, they use the old language. It pulls on you to understand. Without the language we will have to create another way of performing ceremony, a symbolic interpretation.

The songs are next to language in importance but simpler, more permanent. Anyone can learn a song; I know probably one thousand songs. Music is rearranging notes; chants do the same with sounds. A singing voice is an identification mark. My boy will have the same voice I do. People will tell what family he comes from by listening to him sing.

My dad used to say that Indian religion is like a person sleeping. When he inhales, his body gets bigger; when he exhales, it gets smaller—back and forth. When America gets weak maybe Indian religion will become strong. Someday it's going to be important. That's what I think.

Learning something about Indian medicine is good. People who are about my age, those who associate with me, know these things, too. We go to meetings together and sit and talk about it at certain times. We say, "Did you see this?" Or, "Did you feel that? What did you think about it? Okay, let's talk about it." If there are others around, we don't talk about it. Most of the elders are gone now, so it is up to us to discuss these things.

In the Ute language, when people pray to the Holy Spirit, they say, "Let our lives move in the areas where there are spaces." They mean negative spaces, neutral areas—*naria*—a little space here and there. If we must travel through a dangerous area, there must be a path that will be safe. "Let us walk in that little space," we pray. There may be harm, but there will also be a safe space where nothing happens.

Our strong belief is that God is neutral, nature is neutral, but neutral things can turn toward either good or bad. You want to turn always toward the right, the good side; but we have to understand that without the bad there can be no good. So we say, "Even though bad things may happen, let it not be the thing that would hurt us, but the thing that would help us learn or help us appreciate the good." We say it that way. We understand that bad has to happen, but it will always turn to good, too.

2

Early Reservation Days

When my mother was a young girl in Whiterocks, Utah, it was not too many years after her Whiteriver band was moved from Meeker, Colorado. According to the system they were forced to accept on the reservation, they went to pick up rations every Saturday. This was to supplement their diet because their land had been taken away from them, so the government was feeding them.

At this gathering, they would have a big dance. All the Indians would travel there by horseback or in wagons, get there during the day, and then put on their Indian dance outfits. They'd have a big drum and start the music. This dance was not called a pow-wow. *Kunetdavite* they called it, *Kunetdavite*. Saturday. When they left Meeker, they didn't have names for the days of the week, didn't need them. *Kunetdavite* was the day they picked up rations and had the dance. Then they would have the hand games or whatever, too. *Cahchupkdivite*, Friday, was the day to kill a cow for the feast. *Sant* was Sunday, probably taken from Christianity.

One thing that you learn listening to the older group is this: the reservations were structured somewhat like army camps, and so was Fort Duchesne. So when the government set up these Indian boarding schools across the country, they were set up like military schools. Everybody had a uniform. The boys had regular army-type uniforms. The girls would wear dresses that were all the same, their haircuts the same. There was no person greater or lesser—they all looked the same.

An agricultural program was tied in with the school. They'd have the barns and fields, and livestock of all types. They'd produce their own milk with creameries, too; maybe they made their own butter. There were wood shops where they did carpentry work. They had a big boiler where they'd do laundry. They did everything right there. It was run almost the same as a prison camp or an army camp.

Therefore, the punishments given to the students were somewhat severe, like cutting all their hair off so people could tell they were bad or a runaway. They had those kind of things going on. I think it was even worse. They did bodily harm, you might say, to students, taking belts to them, or whips. The teachers would do that. Quite a few Indian students would run away.

When my aunt ran away from the boarding school in Whiterocks, they made her drag a stone sleigh with a rope on it from one end of the school grounds to the other. Then every time she would get to the end, they would put on a boulder. She would have to pull it to the other end; then they would put another boulder on it. Back and forth, every time it would get heavier.

In my mother's day, they took some of the children to school on trains. She was sent to Oregon to a missionary school through the fifth grade. She later came back and got married during World War I. She had bobbed her hair like the flappers who danced the Charleston, and she was the progressive type.

Her parents were part of the Whiteriver band that moved to South Dakota in 1905 to protest the reservation allotment in Utah. Her father had learned the Sioux language and they stayed for several years. They learned the war dance, the lame dance, and the parade and honor songs, and brought them back to the Utes. My mother was born after they returned to Utah, and she lived around Whiterocks all her life.

Clara's father was a somewhat strict person. He would tell her, "Don't ever go into public without washing your face, combing your hair, and putting on something clean." She grew up to be the same way with her children. We had to take a bath and change clothes, and she was washing clothes all the time. She never smoked and would send smokers outside the house. My father would smoke once in a while in the evening. Looking into the west, he'd smoke one cigarette, then place it on the ground. That's the way he was.

My mother was very active in the Episcopal church, but she was doing it for a reason. Beside the chapel was a community building with showers, restrooms, a kitchen, and washing machines. On Sunday she would go to church and have lunch at noon. On Monday and Tuesday she would go back with her laundry. Father Talbot was a good friend of the family and would let her wash clothes there. She would bring her children in to be baptized; she saw it as a trade.

I remember being in the house when my great-grandfather died. John Duncan was one of the last chiefs of the Tumpanawaach-Uintah band. He died in the evening. I remember there was a fire outside the house.

He had a cabin a mile northwest of Whiterocks. The cabin stood north to south with a porch on the east side, where John Duncan lay. On the north side was a bedroom with one bed, and on the south side, a kitchen. I remember the old ladies inside the house. Then there was a loud shrill whistle—two of them. A man came in the room and said something, and the ladies started crying. The whistles had been made by John; his spirit had escaped. I was six years old.

A man from Wyoming named Percy McCloud arrived the next day. He was a young man, though older than my dad, and he was one of John's friends. I remember him clearly. He didn't know my grandfather was even sick. He came to that place and found John Duncan had died. I remember he cried; he cried loud.

Some Indians believe it is bad for someone to die inside a house, but my great-grandfather and great-grandmother were different in this way. My dad would tell how when my great-grandfather took care of him, he told him his experiences a long time ago when they lived in teepees. He was one of the Tumpanawach band, born in the Heber Valley and related to the Shoshones at Fort Hall and Wind River. In the early days in the Fort Bridger area, there was a Shoshone

8

encampment. The Washakie would send their war parties east over the plains to the Arapahoes. Sioux and others would go, and when my great-grandfather and his friend would try to trail them, Old Man Washakie would find out somehow. Since this was a man's world, he would send them back to the encampment.

Teepee ways were different, not because of superstitious beliefs but because of survival techniques the teepee taught. They would get up in the morning before the sun rose. Nobody was supposed to drink water after sunset or before sunrise. There were certain ways to make a fire; certain ways to tie the horses. These restrictions were based on fear, because an enemy could sneak up on them. Then later the people moved into frame houses on the Uintah-Ouray reservation. My great-grandfather said, "When you move from a teepee into a frame house, you leave all of the teepee ways back there. In a frame house you can sleep all you want."

At that time among my people, there was a unity with people coming from Colorado to Utah just two decades back, putting the reservation together. That's not too much time, and there was still a communal feeling—everything belonged to everyone. The social structure was designed for everything to work together. Wherever there was an Indian gathering, there were a lot of Indians present, gambling or playing hand games in the evenings. Even if the gathering was miles away, they would walk over and be there. And at Bear Dance time there would be more people, too, more participants, more Indians. The Sun Dance was the same way; a lot of people came and camped. Everybody stayed there; they didn't go into town to buy this and that. They had nothing to do with town. Very few people went into town. They knew each other; they knew who their relations were. Indians formed a group away from everybody, but a group that was united, too.

Yet later the Utes lived away from people except for family. Family was important. In the 1930s and 1940s the people lived in villages. South of us were a group of the Arreeps and Chimboruses, all belonging to the Whiteriver band. North of us lived the Ice family and the Cornpeach family. They never mixed with us much. When we'd visit them our parents would say, "Don't do this with them. Their way is different."

My parents married at the time when some of the traditional ways were changing. Before then, among some people, certain marriages were not based on love but on arrangements. Certain marriages were communal, owned by the group, arranged by the parents. You would grow up knowing who you would marry, then learn to love them later. For example, if two families were oriented toward the Sun Dance, and one had a daughter and the other a son, they would decide their children would marry and produce Sun Dance followers. If a wife died, her younger sister would often move up and take her place.

Later, when marriage was by individual choice, the parents would tell their boys, in a joking way, "Marry a woman who is a little on the ugly side but who is energetic. Then you will feel free. When you travel you'll know your wife will still be there when you come home. If you marry a pretty one, there will always be someone waiting just outside the door."

They would tell their girls, "Marry someone older than you. He will be more stable than a younger man; he will know how to take care of you. He's not going to beat up on you."

3

The Bear Dance

When I was five or six years old, my mother and father dressed me up in a pair of moccasins, beaded gauntlet gloves, and a small beaded vest and neck ornament. They bought me a small cowboy hat and took me to the Bear Dance.

Certain Bear Dance songs heard around that time were sung about the white people who would attend the Bear Dance and sit in their Model A cars, watching. An Indian made up this song:

> White man sitting in a car.
> The white man is a bragger.
> Now he's sitting in that car.
> I can hear his laughter.
> I can hear his laughter.

In the springtime, when the days got longer the grass began to grow, and leaves and buds sprouted on the trees, it was Bear Dance time. We would all go in a wagon along the little trail that intersected with other trails, arriving at a big flat area. There would be a lot of people there, some came on horseback, some in wagons. This Bear Dance may have been the main social gathering of the year at that time.

Preserved in my memory, the dance begins at about three o'clock in the arbor—the Bear Dance corral made of willows about six feet high has a twenty-foot opening for a door. The circle is about seventy-five to one hundred feet or more in diameter, maybe larger. The men sit on the west side, the ladies on the east side, the singers directly in the center on the west side of the circle. They have an instrument that makes a noise like a bear. A man called the Cat is like a cheerleader, but he pushes people into things, too, kind of controls everything. But he is not the main boss; he is merely working for the main boss. The only thing the boss does is get up and make announcements, talk. Everybody listens when he talks.

The people are dressed appropriately. The ladies wear shawls; the older ones wear a handkerchief or scarf on their heads. The women wear high-top moccasins and dresses. Some have beaded purses, some wear beaded leggings, some have beaded buckskin dresses. The men wear vests, beaded moccasins, and black trousers. Some dress in everyday clothes; some have a long breechcloth hanging down in back. When they dance, it sways.

They sing a beginning song and a closing song; in between they can sing anything they want. The first song is the invitation song, sung for a very short period. The women go up and hit their partners with their shawl fringes, whoever they want to dance with. Then the women come back and form a line facing west; if there are too many, they form a second line, a third line, about a hundred or more women. When the first music stops, they are ready.

The men have to go down to the center and face their partners. The Cat straightens the line, shoulder to shoulder, a straight line. He has a long willow like a whip and hits them on the rear end if they don't hurry.

"Come on!" He hits them hard; it stings, so they run to the center. If the woman finds that the man she picked doesn't move, she tells the Cat, "That man won't dance with me." He goes over there, hits the man real hard, and says, "You get down there." The man gets up without even saying a word; he won't fight back. This goes on for four days—Friday, Saturday, Sunday, and Monday.

So my parents take me over there all dressed up, kind of like a show. I'm the showcase; people will look at me; I'm the one. My father dances, my mother dances, I'm turned loose. Some white people with a box camera take pictures of me beside another boy who is all dressed up.

My grown-up girl cousins say, "Come on, Clifford, dance with us." I hold on to them, going through the motions. I take more steps for their steps, running back and forth. All the motions are one. Everybody's involved, everybody sings. When everybody sings, it really sends out the spirit, picks us up. We are celebrating the coming of spring. We are happy we made it through the winter. We welcome the bears and all the animals.

When a bear wakes from hibernation, he goes for a tree and scratches it. He marks all around the tree, and there is a rhythm to how he's doing this. At the same time, he's singing a song. Everybody steps to that rhythm; the Bear Dance has a little world of its own. Everybody understands that.

That year I had a lot of fun, and people watched me. After two or three years, I outgrew the clothes. Today I still have the vests. My mother pawned the gloves.

A long time ago in the early 1900s, my mother told me, they would have a night dance on the third night of the Bear Dance—dance all night and make fires. In the morning when the sun rose, they would line up the people present and face them east. Then the medicine man held an eagle feather and a special brush. He would pray for all his people and for the spring, the summer, the fall, and the winter. Then everyone would return home, and the head of the household would continue the prayer for his family.

He would talk to all the little things, insects, bugs, snakes, things like that. He would say, "You snakes and bugs, this is where we live. When you're around here, don't bother my kids. Don't scare them. Be friendly with them. You bugs, too. Your land is out there; we have lived here for several years. But we can live together on this world. You live on your land, too." Then he would shake the brush all the way around the house, especially when the children were small, to give them a safe perimeter.

Then on the fourth day, everyone would return to the dance knowing they would have a feast. They bring their pots, dishes, silverware, all stashed away on the wagons. They bring in food and neatly pile it in the middle, waiting with pots, buckets, all the things they're going to use, and they cover all that. They continue the songs and dances, then have the closing song and sing it over and over again. That's when the Cat separates them into couples with their arms over the shoulder. The idea is that the man pushes the woman one way, and the woman pushes the man the other. They can go as far as they want toward the door, then back again, back and forth. The song can last one hour, two hours, until one person falls. Then when one falls, that ends the dance. (You can have a spare stand and watch you; when you're tired, the spare can replace you.)

Finally someone makes a slip and falls, most often a woman. Everyone goes to their seats, and the head singer comes, facing east, and stands over that person. "You're not strong in your knees," he says. "You have to be strong the rest of your life." Then he talks to the Great Spirit, and goes over the person's body, giving strength from that time on to the person.

You can look at this two ways. You can say, "I don't want to fall; I don't like that." Or you can say, "I'd like to fall, to be given a new life, another chance." That's how it was in my mother's time.

Finally they would have a feast, with everybody seated around tablecloths on the ground. The serving would start from the door and move around in a circle. It was all organized, and all these people were disciplined. They were conditioned to this system. For instance, you couldn't talk back to your elders. If an older person came up to you and said, "You're no good; you do this and that," the proper answer was, "Yes, I do those things; you're talking about me. I'm sorry." That's it. You didn't say, "Well, what about you?" Today it's like that; today they would say, "Well, what about you? You've done that, too."

I didn't really think about that disciplinary action until later on, how people began to use different ways of disciplining. And I wondered, did it begin with them? Did it die with the old folks? Did it die because people weren't paying any attention, weren't learning, just figured it would be there the rest of their lives—there would be someone to teach them—and nobody was?

Once, the Bear Dance was a sacred dance, a religious dance. Now it is merely a social dance. It was never a fertility rite, but you read that in books. I look at it this way. There were Mormon dances at the wardhouses, too. Couples would get together there, too, but nobody writes about that. That could happen at the Bear Dance, too, but the Bear Dance wasn't for the purpose of joining people together. Sure, I could meet my girlfriend there. Love does happen at all gatherings of Indians or whites. It wasn't supposed to be that way, but if love happened, it happened there too.

THE BEAR DANCE

Whiterocks, Utah

Bear Dance singers, from left to right: Hank Larose, Kline Myore, Leroy Toponotes, Jensen Jack, Milton Arrats, and Albert Arrats. The drum is a wooden box with a tin top. It represents the sound of the first thunder.

WHITEROCKS, UTAH, MAY 25, 1985

Elaine Rose Colorow, Northern Ute, at the Bear Dance Corral.

WHITEROCKS, UTAH, MAY 25, 1985

The women, from left to right: Melba Appawora, Velma Sireech, and Geneva Kanip Accawanna.
The men, from left to right: Hank Larose, Albert Cornpeach, and Milton Arrats.

Guy Pinnecoose, Ute Elder.

WHITEROCKS, UTAH, MAY 25, 1985

Leroy Toponotes and Jensen Jack, Bear Dance singers.

Guy Pinnecoose, Ute Elder, at the Whiterocks Bear Dance Corral.

MAY 25, 1985

The notched stick is called the Growler. The bone is usually from a young horse,
so his spirit can help the songs be fast and energetic.

4

Early Childhood

I was born April 10, 1933, at 4:20 a.m. in the old hospital at Fort Duchesne, and I grew up a mile east of Whiterocks, close to the old Fort Roubidoux site.

The first few years of my life, my father worked in a Civilian Conservation Corp. camp, building roads in the backwoods. This was one of President Roosevelt's New Deal programs. I remember on Saturdays the different camps would hold movies and dances—I think it was also an assimilation process. I remember going to the movies, riding in a truck once with a lot of people.

When my parents married, my mother already had my brother Rudolph from a former marriage. He was three years old when I was born, and I believed he was always her favorite boy. I had some problem with my right knee—something like arthritis—so that I didn't walk until I was two or three. Now that I am a man, I think she is proud of me. But then I think she believed I would be very difficult to raise.

Because of my handicapped knee, I rode a horse long before I could walk. My dad would put me on with him. Later I rode at a full gallop, standing on the saddle like a trick rider. Elvina was born after me, the sister who died, then my brother Clinton, then Madeline. The others came later on, thirteen of us altogether.

My mother would say, "Clifford," and I would say, "Yes, Clara?" My father was named Ivan. Right from the start, Indian children were treated like small adults. Only now do I say, "my mother," "my dad." My father was an unemotional type of man. We could never quite tell if he loved us or not.

My mother's family had more Indian doctors than my father's side. My parents believed in the Indian way, but they didn't force us to believe their way. This was during the Depression years, and they were mainly concerned with providing for the family. After working at the camp, my dad earned a dollar a day as janitor at the Whiterocks Boarding School. He was paid once a month at the end of the month, thirty dollars. I think about that today, how he walked more than a mile to work. His mind was motivated to the point that he had to do that; it was a responsibility deeply embedded in him.

Since he was a janitor, he would tell us, "I'd rather see you kids work in an office so you don't have to do the things I do." Or he would point to someone sitting in front of the store. "Look at him sitting at the store. He sits waiting for something to happen, for oil money to come. What if it never happens? He's going to sit there for the rest of his life. You've got to get out and work and earn what you need to use. You have to do it on your own."

Our house was divided between a kitchen on the east and a bedroom on the west. There was a wood stove in each room and one bed in the bedroom. We children slept on a mattress on the floor. We rolled it out each night and rolled it back up in the morning. We fetched water from a quarter mile away, where there were several springs.

There was a sharing of duties. My younger brother, Clinton, and I would each take two buckets and haul water every day while Rudolph, who was older, cut wood. He would cut enough to supply that night and the next day until evening. In the winter, we would take a milk can on a sled to the spring, with two pulling and one pushing. After school we would come home and do our chores. Winter was a busy time for us, trying to supply water and fuel. We had no electricity, so we used a kerosene lamp. Later, my dad bought a Coleman lamp. It was bright; it really lit up the old cabin.

In the winter, nights were long. They would tell Coyote stories to make the nights short. There were stories for the way the world was created, how they set down rules such as how many days per year.

The sun was once a mean person that wasn't tamed down until cotton rabbit shot the sun with his arrows. The sun burned a spot on the back of cotton rabbit's neck. Such were the stories.

My parents would sit around the kitchen table and we would say, "Tell this one." There were long stories and short stories, and songs went with every story—a song about a whirlwind around the teepee after the fire has gone out; the wind blew under the teepee like a cold-blooded bird from the north; or a song about the reflection of a sunrise in a red flower. Animals had songs, too. The songs held everything together, like a dream you remember years after you dream it, weaving the past and present. Some songs had words, and there would be very old Ute words preserved in the stories. My dad would tell the stories and my mother would listen with a remark or an addition. With a storyteller, there is always someone there to make corrections so the story will never change.

We didn't have a refrigerator, and so our meals were pretty similar. Our bread was oven-baked although there was a store in Whiterocks. Sometimes we kept chickens and gathered the eggs, or we bought them from a nearby farmer.

We learned that your spirit develops freely if you grow up away from everybody and play with your brothers and sisters and cousins. The world is your playground. You have your own swimming place, and you know nobody is going to be there when you arrive. You know you are beyond your limits when you go somewhere and someone else is there.

As boys we pretended to hunt and we made bows and arrows. We figured out which wood to use and whittled it down. We sharpened nails and tied feathers on the back. We each had a bow and arrows for hunting. We wanted it to be realistic, so we decided the horses could pretend to be our elk. Those horses ran, but the nails hung in there. Luckily, none of the horses died.

We played animals, too, mountain lion or horse, looking for water. We would kick and move like that animal, learn to think like the animal. Later when we went deer hunting, we knew how to think like a deer. We knew where a deer would be hiding, how it would watch for us.

We had a swimming hole where the water was deep and the trees thick. We cleaned the brush away and built diving boards. We put ropes in the trees to swing like Tarzan in the movies, then drop into the water. We made tunnels through the thickets to crawl under the brush. Sometimes I wonder if the tunnels are still there.

Sometimes we pretended we were going to have a Sun Dance. We made whistles and ornaments, then dressed up. We cleared some land and placed a cow skull on a tree like a buffalo skull. We turned a tub upside down for a drum. Then we'd sing and begin the ceremony. We knew the songs even then. Sometimes we got the girls to sing, too.

I was a shabby image of a skinny little boy in coveralls, hair standing up wrong, the back part of me dipping in. As I grew up, if my siblings wanted someone to blame for stealing cookies or oranges that were hidden, someone would say, "Clifford did it," and I would take the punishment. In those days, punishment wasn't a parent sitting down and talking to you, but taking a belt to you.

If parents wanted to buy you something, they chose. The child had no choice. Sometimes I really envied people who had money. They could buy shoes for their kids, the kind the children liked—low-cut oxfords. My dad would say, "No, we can't buy them. They won't last long. You buy high-top shoes."

"Okay." That was it.

My father also had a favorite son; it wasn't me. So I grew up that way, a weakling too. Kids my age were strong. If they wanted to pick on someone, they'd jump on me, beat the hell out of me. They knew they could beat me because I was too skinny to fight back.

I remember walking to the school or to the store one time, along the trail. Some kids were hiding along the way. Finally they came out. "Hey, you want to fight?"

They hit me in the face. I was crying. But I turned and went home.

I said, "Oh, I had an accident." I knew the people who did it; they were strong and older than me, too.

That feeling inside me built, not like hate but like revenge. I wished to be like Superman, take off my shirt and stand there with a big *S* on my chest. Or like Captain Marvel—Shazaam! Then I would fly up and beat the hell out of them, throw them up in the sky. So I lived with that. I guess as years went by, I began to find that the strong became weak, but I still maintained my level.

Then one day somebody told me, "You have a good mind, you're different. You should develop your thinking."

I thought, "Okay, fine."

A teacher said, "You are very good at mathematics." The teacher could give me any kind of mathematical problem and I could solve it.

We wrote an essay one time. My topic was the weather; the falling snow. The words I wrote were these: "The world has a white coat it puts on every year. It has put on the coat again."

The teacher said, "You know, that's good. That's where you're different."

This was during my second year of school. The boarding schools had a disciplinary feeling to them, a military technique to teach Indians discipline. School was used for assimilation purposes. They didn't allow us to talk Indian languages on the grounds. If students ran away from the school, they were severely punished. At that time there was still this idea that being sent away to school was to assimilate.

I remember in fourth grade, the school took some Indian children to Salt Lake City on a trip. My father and I rode with them. The group we came in with was made up all of girls, and I was the only boy sitting among them. Coming into Heber, everyone was excited because they could see the image of a woman on Mt. Timpanogos. I had a problem of visualizing, so I didn't see it.

Father and I stayed at the Wilson Hotel, and it was then we bought our first family car from Streator-Smith's Chevrolet. When I got home I wrote an article for the school paper, which was named *Psedenie* (To Tell a Story). My article described a machine that you get into and close the door, which goes *ssssshhhh*. Then a man pushes a lever and the machine goes up, and you get off on another floor. I drew a sketch of this machine, an elevator.

When I was ten years old, we moved to the Fort Duchesne community. That was something new, because only a small percentage of the students in the public school were Indians. My teacher was a white woman named Mrs. Burgess, and two grades met in one room. For a time I was self-conscious about being Indian.

Mrs. Burgess noticed that I could draw and sketch. It seemed to me that all Indian children were artistic. She used to have me do sketches. Our class was making watch fobs for the Veterans Hospital in Salt Lake City, and so she asked me to draw Indian designs on them. I wasn't sure what she meant by Indian designs, but I tried to please her.

Meanwhile in school we all had to learn the waltz and the foxtrot. Mrs. Burgess would play a song on the piano, and we had to dance with a partner. When there were no Indian girls to dance with, I had to dance with a white girl. I was careful not to get very close.

I was cautious because my dad used to bring the family to Salt Lake City to visit a relative in the old Sugar House prison. Vines grew on the side of the prison and, with its high rock walls, it really looked like a prison. My mother would wait with us while my father went inside. Finally he would come back out and say, "He's getting along all right."

Father told me, "Clifford, our relative is in there because he went with a white girl. The law says you're not supposed to do that, and he did. That's why he's in prison. I don't want you to ever do that."

The car my father bought in Salt Lake City took us out of our little world. We went to Wind River, Wyoming, and to Idaho to meet relatives. My mother had been to Fort Washakie in Wyoming, north of Lander. She had relatives there. As we drove, she remembered the trails they had followed when she was a girl, and the stops the horses made. At midpoint, she told us, men on horseback would ride into town to buy groceries for the camp.

After living three years in Fort Duchesne, we moved back to Whiterocks. I was used to public school by then, so I decided to attend eighth grade at the public school in Tridell. During my teenage years the reservation would change. I would learn the ways of the modern American side.

Looking back on my life, I think of how I came into this world and of these very first impressions that put the outside world into me. These early experiences, shaped through the years, put me together into what I am now.

5

Indian Religion

As teenagers in school, we kept Indian religion in our back pocket because of ridicule, the downplaying of Indian religion by society. But boys from traditional families stuck together.

When I was a young child, an Arapaho hitchhiker named Carlos Star stayed with my family. He was an older person, the same age as my dad. He was a peyoteist. I would listen to him sing with the drum and the gourd. He spent some time with us, and he also attended ceremonies among his own people. So one day he went back to Oklahoma. When he left, he told my parents, "Before I leave, I'm going to give these feathers to this boy." He laid them on my chest while I was asleep, and my mother put the feathers away for me. Recently I passed on those feathers to my grandson, Kyri.

Then, when I was in my early teens, two Arapahos, Henry Tyler and Joe Antelope, stayed with us. They did our usual chores for their keep, cutting wood and hauling water. Also they would sing, and sometimes my older cousins would show up to sing with them. I sat nearby and listened. One evening they were going to a meeting. I decided that this one time I would go with them. It was wintertime. We walked covered with our blankets a mile or two through the moonlight on the icy trail. Our steps were noisy.

When we were in the meeting, I remember two women singing that night. Later I learned that when World War II ended and the men returned, the women no longer sang. I sat in the meeting and listened until the music reached for me. At that time, it selected me, took me for itself. I had transcended over into its world.

I was interested in exploring this world, and in the spring I decided to go to the Bear Dance. Maybe I could find a friend to dance with, or at least a girl to hold on to as we danced.

At this dance I was not a cute little boy dressed up in beads and a cowboy hat. I was so skinny that I looked like the children in magazine ads, asking you to send money to help the poor. I combed my hair, but it still stuck up like a haystack, and I was quite shy. I sat on the boys' side and waited for the ladies and girls to cross the square and hit us with their shawl fringes. Pretty soon I was the only one remaining on the stand. No one hit me in several rounds. So I moved over to the singing group and thought I could sing with them. All around me, men and boys were chosen and got up to dance. Pretty soon I was the only one singing.

I made up my mind that no one was going to choose me. Nobody wanted me. The heck with it. I walked away from the Bear Dance. I took that disappointment with me, carrying it always. To this day, I don't dance the Bear Dance.

Around that time my family went to Idaho to visit the Bannocks and Shoshone people. And in the evening my father and I went into a teepee meeting. The person conducting the meeting was a Sioux elder named Oscar Two Eagle. All were sitting in a circle with the chief on the west, facing east. We sat on the north side. The singing commenced and the drum went around, with each person singing four songs.

I listened for a while, then leaned toward my father. "I'd like to sing."

"Yeah?"

"Yeah."

"You know any songs?"

"Yes, I know some songs."

"Okay. Sing only four now. When you get through the fourth, pass the drum on to that man next to you."

"All right." I sang my four songs. That was my beginning.

In the morning I overheard Ivan telling the chief that was the first time I had ever sung in a meeting. He laughed and said, "No, I don't think so. That boy has been in a meeting before."

I explain it this way: a person can have religion built in, not from teachings but from living it. It's not performing, showing what you have learned, but doing what you have learned to live. Within a ceremony, I have never felt unwanted. The ceremony and all it contained was only between me and my creator.

6

The Other Side

About this time I began to think about what I wanted to do with the rest of my life. When we were young, my brothers and I were roughnecks. We were close to nature because we were dirty; you can't get any closer. My uncle would show up in a nice shirt; he looked good. My mother would talk about how her brother had gone to school at Haskell Institute, an Indian school in Lawrence, Kansas. A lot of kids had been sent to Haskell, and others to Salem, Oregon, where my mother went. Haskell was a vocational school. My uncle became a painter, so that's why he lived in a better world and made good money. He'd talk about the football players he'd seen play at the University of Kansas and at Haskell.

I liked that; I liked the stories. He said he met the man who modeled for the Indian head nickel, a Sioux who visited Haskell and talked to the students. I really wanted to go to the Haskell Institute.

One day I talked to Roy Adams, the principal at the boarding school in Whiterocks. He was responsible for sending kids beyond the ninth grade level, away to school in Riverside, California, or Phoenix. I went to him and said, "I'd like to go to school—to Haskell. I really want to go to school there."

He said, "No, you have access to a school bus. You can get on the school bus and go to school in Tridell or Roosevelt. So, therefore you cannot go to Haskell."

That was the final word.

Often parents would go to him and say, "My child would like to go to school somewhere else." Sending kids away to school might have been a disciplinary mechanism, or a way of keeping them out of their parents' hair so they wouldn't be bothered. My desire to go to Haskell was strictly my own idea. I didn't ask my dad or my mother to talk to the principal. Most Indian children seemed to rely on their parents to do their talking for them, and that continued, sometimes into their adulthood.

After the principal turned me down, I thought about it and realized that every community had a school provided within the reservation, but still they sent students away. Students who lived right on the bus line went away to Haskell. Then how come they wouldn't let me go? At that point, I said the heck with it.

From then on I didn't give a darn about school, though I attended Altara High School for those three years until Union High School opened in Roosevelt. I graduated from Union in the first senior class. I'd sit in the back row and just keep up with the class.

In my late teens there followed a lost period of time, where I said, "Well, I'll just live day to day." At times like that, you're reaching out to almost anything; you have no plans. I come from a good family, my mother, my father. Yet when I got to be about seventeen or eighteen, somehow I didn't appreciate the good compared with things on the other side. So I went on the other side, and I lived with some relatives in Whiterocks. They drank—the children, the mother, the father—and had fun. That's what I wanted, and that's where I made my mistake because that was not life. Now those people are all gone. That's why I had to ease back on to the other side.

Throughout those young years, I balanced the Indian way and the white way. I had to try out a lot of strategies. I knew I would find difficulty because I listened to one of my uncles. He said, "Clifford, you take a white boy and yourself. The white boy lives in the city; you live in the country. You go to school somewhere together. You must always keep this in mind: you are like a person going uphill because you have to climb a mountain. The white boy doesn't have to climb a mountain; his road is level, straight. The white boy has parents who associate with different individuals, a banker, a construction worker. It's easier for that boy to find a job because his parents will say, 'Why don't you go ask him for a job?' Or a friend will say, 'Why don't you come work for me?'

"It's going to be hard because they are not going to say that to you. You're going uphill, so that's why you have to study a little bit harder than the white boy. You're going to make it, but you've got to realize that you'll be going uphill all the way. It's not going to level off."

That's what my uncle said, and I agree with him. But when you reach the top of that hill, you're all right.

Change on the Reservation

They say that life is divided into four sections: childhood; then youth up to twenty-seven, twenty-eight, or thirty; then adulthood until sixty or seventy; and then old age. When you get to a different stage, you have to adjust for that, adjust the way you eat, the way you live. If you study people, you're going to find it to be this way: Some people will be kids all their lives. They never grow up because they never adjust. Some people will be adults in their earlier years because they adjust sooner. Being twenty-one does not necessarily make one an adult.

When I look at things from that high level, I would speak of my people this way: as a whole, we are still like a young kid. Somewhere we stopped growing, and I think we stopped growing when we started having fun, when the money and alcohol were open. We are still at that level.

At the end of World War II, around 1945 until after 1950, things began to change on the Uintah-Ouray Reservation. During my teenage years, the social structure changed among the Utes, and the changes came fast.

One change developed because, during wartime, people from the reservation were taken to Tooele to work in a smelter. Families spent several years there, away from the reservation, then they returned. It was the beginning of a mix into the outer society.

When the service boys returned from the war, they, too, had experienced a different way of life. Organizations such as the American Legion had posts near Fort Duchesne for veterans. Veterans were highly regarded by the Indian people because they were warriors. Whatever the veterans did was okay.

Liquor was not allowed on the reservation then, and Indian people themselves were under restriction. They could not drink. If you were caught drinking, you were put in jail. So the veterans fought for the right to drink, the right to have alcohol on the reservation, not only here but elsewhere in Indian country. The soldiers had been exposed to this. In the service they could do whatever they wanted; they could drink with the other soldier boys. They began to enjoy the idea of drinking.

The groups that returned from Tooele supported that idea, too, because they had learned to live that way away from reservation. Now they wanted to bring drinking to the reservation, introduce it to their people. Of course there had always been a few people who drank and would go off the reservation to buy their liquor, then come back. But now the laws and attitudes changed, and a drastic change in the lifestyle of my people started at that point.

So alcohol brought one kind of change and money brought changes, too. By 1955 the Land Claims Commission was in full operation, compensating the Utes for land losses in Colorado. This is the federal government giving money away through the proper channels. The tribe received a lot of money, $37 million, and things began to move in a different direction with money available and alcohol flowing free.

At the same time, people were talking about development—they wanted to build a recreation hall, have scholarships, set up the students. They programmed their expenditures. The tribe takes so much, and the individuals are given so much in dividends. Then they systemized the dividends into a ten-year program: you're going to buy this, buy that, this is for your home. If you want a car, you have to be approved by a board. All of that was happening.

They didn't give you the money. They gave you a purchase order. You would get what you wanted, and the store would get reimbursed.

That's when Indian people would buy, say, a television for a $300 purchase order, and then sell it to a white man for $150 so they could get cash. They fought the system, but that's how they fought it. A lot of car dealers, too, would sell bad cars to Indians for purchase orders. So the Indians would lose money. That's how it worked. So all this was happening between 1945 and 1955.

During those years, the question of separating the mixed-bloods was raised, too, but the problem had existed before that time. Mixed-blood ancestry had been accepted by tribal peoples with the idea that offspring would marry into the tribe and be part of the tribe. But it didn't seem to work that way. The offspring usually married away from the tribe.

A good study of the history of the reservation would show that most of the ancestors of the so-called mixed-bloods were Navajos, Paiutes, or maybe some Shoshones, and in most cases they were totally white. They drifted in either with the fur traders, or were taken by the Utes when they raided tribal villages and brought people back. Some may not have had any Ute blood, but in the 1950s they were saying they were Utes. The real beginning of that situation may be that the majority were not; some may not even have had Indian blood. Certain white families came in and said, "Why don't we become a part of you?" and were accepted by the people. Some were like that, too.

These so-called mixed-bloods knew what was going on because they understood the white person, they understood English because of what they were, whereas the Indians were always in the back seat. So when any opportunities came along, the mixed-bloods would be there first—job opportunities and so on. They worked in the office that was established for the Indians, and so they had information.

The Indians held back with the idea that the mixed-bloods might just go away. That hope never materialized the way they thought; still, when the chance came to terminate tribes with the Indian Reorganization Act of 1934, the Utes accepted it in 1937 and used the law to move the mixed-bloods away, but with certain privileges extended just to them. Then the Indians could move into the front seat and take off from there, gaining the opportunity to do something for themselves.

The big picture the mixed-bloods were looking at was this: when they were terminated, they got a large sum of money plus land. Also, along with this came a program to educate them; so certain ones took advantage of it by going to the universities.

The way Indian people look at the situation is that the mixed-bloods were paid off—and then they had nothing else to do with tribal rights. That's it. Actually, we gave them money for something we were not quite clear about; the question was how they became mixed-bloods or Affiliated Utes.

Prior to 1955 they would rather stand on the other side of the fence, laughing and pointing at "those people over there" because there were no benefits to being an Indian. But when the federal programs and the money came in, they wanted to be Indian. All at once you find Sun Dancers among the mixed-bloods.

So during those years we were having fun, and on the other hand, we were trying to make an adjustment. Maybe we were losing all our old ways, too. Losing the Indian ways began somewhere at that point when we had money and alcohol was available on the reservation. Education-wise, things began to change, too. The lifestyle of the Indians changed really fast. The changes began to pick up momentum, and here we are today.

For one thing, there was a change in the way people looked at chiefs. You did the thing the chief wanted you to do out of respect for the person, respect that was slowly built as the chief conducted his life. The person who had the most respect became chief because people would do things because they liked him. The chief was not a hero; people get the wrong idea. But that's gone, too, now. For instance, now we have the council system but it's oriented to having power over people. We become invisible people.

If you compare the leaders we had prior to that time and the way they conducted business with today's leaders, there is quite a difference. The older people—no matter if they were uneducated—were wise. What they said, what they brought out, was true; everything they did was for the people. When they talked, people would listen. If they disagreed on an issue, they would talk about it and then compromise; that's how they did business. They had a pretty good idea in what direction they were heading. Now when you look at the leaders—no matter if they might be educated—that one thing is missing. They are not mature. They don't take issues to the point of decision while still showing respect for each other; that quality is not there.

The attitudes people have today about leaders, cooperation, how people live, are all different. At that time people lived out in the country, but now you find groups of houses. I think the federal government had a lot to do with that, too, through the housing programs.

Today a leader may get chosen this way: "I'll help you when I get into the council." He goes around telling people that. In fact, he may give money to get votes so that he'll get in. His concern may be just to get in there to get a big salary, but he makes sure he gives donations here and there to the people he promised. He'll give them jobs sometimes, or money to pay their utilities. The rest of the people to him— or to her—are not present, they're invisible. He doesn't give a darn about developing programs unless they are beneficial for him. In fact, he could be a type who doesn't know anything, really.

But the older chiefs who started working on the council back in the 1930s and 1940s, they were the type who looked after everything. Everybody was their concern, and they wanted to make sure the government treated them right. Their minds were a little different; they were broad-minded people. They were trying to work with the Bureau of Indian Affairs, trying to figure out what "big brother" was doing. They were formulating the government they later would have.

In 1934 when the Indian Reorganization Act came about—when it was accepted in 1937 by the Utes—the bylaws they created fit the situation. But today the bylaws have not changed too much. If we could close some of the loopholes and separate responsibilities to establish the checks and balances we don't have now, tribal government would work well. The attitudes have changed, the value systems have changed, but the bylaws haven't changed. As things change, the system begins to develop loopholes. That's where we are.

8

Indian Rodeo

About the time I was a senior in high school, I got interested in rodeo. My great-grandfather John Duncan, during his travels in the early part of the century, had journeyed back East. While he was there, he bought some thoroughbred mares and had them shipped to Salt Lake City, then hauled on a truck to the Uintah Basin. He bred them with mustang stallions and came up with a fine-featured horse with a heavy body. They were good-looking horses.

When he died, some of the horses went to my dad. We'd have roundup time in the spring for about seventy head to corral, brand, and castrate. My dad was careful to see that they didn't inbreed. He was very good with horses. My great-grandfather had cattle, too, but my father worked all day and didn't want cattle. He said cattle are like babies. Horses are more independent. Cattle won't dig down through the snow for food the way horses will.

As a very young boy, I learned to ride with the horse, not against it. My dad had some books about horses. One was by Will James, a cowboy artist and writer. I read about a horse named Smokey. My dad used to rodeo, then later did calf roping. He had friends who were professional ropers, and that's where he picked up my name. There was a steer roper named Clifford Helm, so my parents named me Clifford Helm Duncan.

With the beginning of the oil revenues that were paid to tribal members, we went to Pendleton, Oregon, for the roundup. We took in the rodeo and all the Indian activities. I entered an Indian dance contest with the fancy war dance, and I took fourth place out of hundreds of dancers. They gave me a Pendleton blanket.

While we were there, I bought a regulation saddle for saddle bronc contests. Before, I had just borrowed saddles, but this one was custom-made. At the Duchesne rodeo that fall, I won third place, so I started competing in other rodeos. My dad said bareback was easier for him than saddle bronc, but for me it was the opposite.

Saddle bronc riding is a matter of balance. You stay with the horse by shifting your weight. A horse is like all things in that it has a pivot point. The top of its shoulder stays level as it bucks. You put the saddle on top of the pivot point; it's made to fit only that one place. You push it up there with your leg, then tighten it down.

Never look a horse in the eye because it can figure you out; it can tell if you're afraid. Keep your eyes averted or it will start treating you rough.

Horses are a lot like people in the way they follow the leader, except for one or two mavericks. You study the mavericks, make a wide turn to get ahead of them, then cut them off. When you learn how people move, it's like watching horses.

One time there were some white boys from Lapoint who rode to Whiterocks to break in their horses. They saw six or seven of us by the corral and came over to talk.

"Do you have any good bucking horses we can ride?" they asked. "Maybe we can bet."

"I'll make a bet I can outride you," I told one of them.

"Okay."

"I'll make it easy on you. You can have first choice of the horses."

"Okay."

We watched the horses running around. He picked out a good-looking one. There was a mean-looking one that would spook at anything. "I'm going to ride that one," I told him.

The white boy went in first, saddled the horse, and rode him as he bucked all the way down the corral. Down at the end, he was bucked off.

I saddled the spooky horse, and we took off into the ring like a dancing couple. I stayed with him as he bucked until they blew the whistle. When I shouted, "Whoa," and the horse stopped. He stood still. I rode him back to the chute where the boys were all laughing.

"You tricked us," my competitor said.

"Yeah, I was just teasing you guys."

9

Military Service

After I graduated from high school, I was drafted into the army during the Korean War. They had us fill out forms in the army. One question asked, "Are you a native born American?" I checked "yes."

Then it asked, "Have you ever learned a foreign language?" Again I checked "yes."

"If yes, what language?" it asked.

"English," I wrote.

After my training at Fort Ord, I came home on leave before being sent overseas. I had to catch a bus in Roosevelt, about eight. I packed my duffle bag, and the whole family drove me down. Finally the bus pulled in, and they loaded my duffle bag. I got on, and they punched my ticket. I went back and sat down. Then I looked up and found my dad had followed me on. He talked to me. Then he went out.

All the years I had been with my father, he had never shown any feeling toward his children. But when I was going away, then I knew. Still, it was kind of a bad time to feel that emotion because I was leaving, and there was no time to appreciate it. It was a strong moment I had with my dad; just a few words, and love shoots right through you, Indian love. Then he goes out. The Indian way is strong at that moment.

Going into the service had to be done because others were doing it; this was part of the world we were living in. My parents accepted that; they were that kind of people. Going into the service is something that differs with each family group among Indians. Some people will say, "Well, you're going to be killing all of them. You're going to be a great warrior." Others will say, "This war is not your fault. The white people are causing problems. You don't have to go." And others say, "Well, okay, go over; and without losing too much time, you'll soon be free again." In each family it's different. I notice, too, that going in the service, going to war, is kind of like being a hero.

When I went into the service, the hardest part of going away after living on the reservation was moving from one world to another so fast—and with the idea that you might not even come back. In the army they told me, "You are now a professional killer. We've been training you to be a professional killer."

Here I was, an Indian boy. In Indian culture, growing up on the reservation, you have no orientation to kill anybody. In fact, you're taught not to kill anybody. So that was one battle—how would I deal with that?

I felt vulnerable, lonely. I tried to find something I could associate with home. One of the things I found was the Mormon Church, familiar from the Uintah Basin. There were three or four boys who were Mormon.

"Can I go to church with you guys?"

"Sure."

So we went. There were a lot of boys at the church. The person in charge—the bishop, or whoever—said, "Well, we have new boys here. Will you please stand up and introduce yourselves to the congregation? At the same time, you can tell us what branch or what ward you're from."

I wanted to play that role, too. I got up (here, I wasn't even a Mormon), and I said, "I belong to the Whiterocks Ward in Whiterocks, Utah."

"Fine," he said. That was it.

In reality, I was just lonesome, but the Mormon Church was what I grew up knowing. I liked the songs they'd sing, the old pioneer songs. I think a lot of Indians are that way. We go to church as long as we can please the other person. Then at some point we say, "Well, I don't want to do that. I want this Indian way." I think most of us travel that road, but we have respect for those religions. If they are going to do good for someone, fine. But for me, it's got to be this other side because I associate myself with religion in a different way.

In my family we don't talk about what we did during our military service. If you talk about it, you own those things you did.

I came out of the service in June 1955. I had been exposed to drinking, so now I would go with the crowd. I did that for a couple of years. Eventually I would slow down and say, "This is not the way to live," and stop, but I didn't stop totally. Every once in a while I would drink for some time, and then quit and get on with my life again.

During those years from 1945 to 1955, things appeared to be all right on the reservation. We were living in a cloud of dust. When the dust settled, we seemed to be all right; then the dust would rise again. What wasn't exposed was the reality that we were actually going downhill. We were on a slope, picking up momentum as we went downhill.

10

The Sun Dance

In July or August, after my return from military service, I went into the Sun Dance for the first time. I wasn't ready for it.

The Sun Dance, which came from the Shoshone tribe in the late 1800s, is a sacred ceremony connected to the warrior life. If you Sun Dance you become a kind of warrior. If you're in combat, or in a situation where you might be up against other Indians, you will always win. Arrows will not harm you. The Sun Dance is a shield to protect you.

So when you are involved in that kind of ceremony, you have a lot of rules and regulations to follow. If you make a slip somewhere, it signifies you are going to get hurt because you did not do things right. If a group of people watched you when that slip happened, they will later say, "I knew that would happen because of what he said—or did—in that ceremony. With the Sun Dance you watch everything you do and say. You've got to be careful who you talk to, all of that.

There has been quite a lot of change within the Sun Dance lodge since 1955, also outside of it. One of the biggest changes has been in attitude. Recently I was in a Sun Dance, and the chief was a young man. He was one of those who like to be greater than the next one: "I'm the one. I'm it. Here I am." Instead of using twelve poles in the Sun Dance lodge, he used three. He said, "I'm the one who's doing it. If there's any person who wants to question my ways, let him come and stand right here before me."

That's what he said. From that Sun Dance to the next a year later, he was gone—dead. A car hit him. When it happened, my mind

flashed back to that time: "If there's anybody who wants to say something about it, let him come here before me and say it."

The Sun Dance is a complex world. You've got to watch when
going in and out; you've got to watch who you go in front of so you
don't block anyone. Keep young babies away from the Sun Dance.
Keep pregnant women away from the Sun Dance; keep menstruating
women away from the Sun Dance.

When you're talking about spiritual powers, they say the eagle
is the most powerful bird, beyond any animal. There's another hawk
behind the eagle. I have a set of feathers my sister gave me to use.
We treat the feathers reverently. The bird can be contaminated. In
the Ute way, you don't let blood touch a feather. If the bird touches
that blood, it's contaminated from the outside. Because women have
menstrual periods every month, they are somewhat associated with
blood, so they can't touch sacred objects. That's why they keep away
from the Sun Dance grounds at the time of their menstrual periods. It
doesn't mean they are inferior; it just means they are different.

Women have a power; women have a special place in this life. In
certain ceremonies a time will come when a man will say, "This area,
close to sunrise, is a woman's place." The most sacred place in the
world belongs to a woman. God is going to listen to you at that time.
You're the one who is going to speak for the rest of the people; new
day, new life, new sunrise.

Women bring life into the body, so it ties into nature. Women are
not inferior, but the way people write it, it sounds like the Indian man
is superior. He isn't. Women have a special place that is connected to
certain birds, certain animals, a certain time of day. The sicknesses
that women go through will come, then go away again. You can talk to
the sun if you make up your mind, the spirit of light, the spirit of the
sun. You can say, "I have this way about me. I want you to help me."
It's wide open to women. That's how we look at it.

The cycle of blood changes the chemistry of what's going on, for
blood is connected to the earth. Animals sense that in ordinary life;

everything changes. When you have been dancing without food and water for several days, you know it, too. There are other rules. You cannot take pictures with a camera. The dancers should stay away from sex or any physical contact with any woman beforehand, and for one month thereafter. In the old days, that's what they did. Now the rules are still there. It's up to you whether you want to pick them up and live by them.

It used to be that on the last day of the Bear Dance, the chief would make the announcement the people were waiting to hear. At that time they had several Sun Dance chiefs. He would point out the chiefs: this one, that one, and name the times, July or whenever. Then everyone would start getting ready.

About a week or two before the Sun Dance, the chief moves to the Sun Dance grounds and sets up his camp. He selects the spot where the Sun Dance tree will be placed, marks off a circle, and sticks willow into the ground. Those are the boundaries; the camp sites are to be outside the circle. Certain bands have areas, such as the Uncompahgre on the south side, the White Rivers over there, the Uintahs here. Way back there is an area where they will have a stand to sell coffee, food. Then the other tribes come and camp too.

The chief locates a Sun Dance tree, a sacred center pole. He marks that; he knows where it is. When the time draws close, he goes and cuts that tree. In the meantime people are moving in. They get long poles that will lean in a circle—the lodge poles. They leave early one morning, several horse-drawn wagons, and go to the mountains while it's still dark. You can hear the chief's wife making the *caruhruh*—a sound associated with power, spirit. (I have heard that sound used by other nationalities, such as Arabians.) This is a spiritual medicine sound, given a special power. The ladies use this sound; it's loud, and all who want to join in like the birds.

Then the sun rises upon the usual camp activities. But someone is always watching. When the wagons arrive in the mountains, a fire will be built. When the smoke rises and is seen back at the camp, the women start the *caruhruh* again. Everyone in the camp makes preparations for the Sun Dance.

When the wagons are ready to return, they make a fire again, and again the *caruhruh* is heard. As the wagons rumble toward camp, the *caruhruh* rises again. The center pole is left just outside the camp. Later, designated people on horseback ride swiftly toward the center pole and shoot an arrow to kill that spirit. This also depicts a warrior going out to fight, and there's a special song to sing with that.

Then they would have a parade, dressed in their fineries, riding their finest horses. Everyone sings the parade song, the one they used to sing for warriors coming home. The ladies wear their husbands' war bonnets, and some cry because their warriors didn't return home, they're dead. They have songs for those people.

Meanwhile they move the pole to the center, stopping four times. Then they have a special prayer and lift the pole four different times and hold it, then return it to the ground. Each time they lift it a little bit higher. The fourth time they lift it straight up. Then they place the twelve poles and run them to the center. So the construction begins and has to be completed that day.

The families are all ready, and the chief is camped in the back of the Sun Dance corral. On the center pole is the buffalo skull, facing west. All the dancers will be on the west side, Everyone looks about the same—an eagle-bone whistle and maybe a breast ornament, a shawl covering from the waist on down.

Over by the chief's shade-house is a teepee, and the dancers are going to have a special prayer in that teepee. There's going to be a bucket of water; there is a prayer for that water, and then the partaking of water. The sun dancers are ready to go in.

The chief goes in first, and he goes clockwise around the arbor three times, signifying the dance will be three nights. You know by the circle how many days you'll be in there, without food, without water. If he goes four, you know that you're going to get out Tuesday evening, and this is Friday. If he goes three, you'll be out on Monday. Then you're in.

The Sun Dance was the only ceremony to ever give me a hard time. It was the first time I was in a ceremony for three days and three nights. Soon afterward I took part in three more Sun Dances, one each year. I didn't know how to Sun Dance. The only thing I knew how to do was stand up and blow the eagle-bone whistle. I just stood there.

When you're young, your sincerity at ceremonies is somewhat based on how other people look at you. If they accept you, you're part of it. If they laugh at you, then you don't want any part of it. It's like the peer groups in school today; if they do it, you do it. In ceremonies where everyone comes, it's like that.

Eventually when that changes, you find that the peer group really had no effect on your life. They had nothing to do with your life to begin with, and nothing to do with it thereafter except to be there. Later you put them aside. You think, "They don't do anything for me anyway. Why should I worry about them? I can do anything in front of them; they can go ahead and laugh." You always find that eventually they are with you; you broke away from them but they come back to you and follow you. But if you don't break away, you are following them. You never get away from them. If you become a person who is doing things on his own, eventually you find that people want to be like you.

Anyway, after those first few Sun Dances, I talked to my dad. He had gone into the Sun Dance once in his lifetime. Prior to going into Sun Dance he had severe headaches. One day the elders suggested he Sun Dance and ask God to help, he told me. He had a vision of a buffalo on the prairie and a far-off pond. The buffalo was between him and the pond. He wanted to go around the buffalo and get a drink, but there was no hiding place. Finally, he did get his drink in the vision. He came out of the Sun Dance and didn't have headaches anymore.

"I didn't go there for fun or to show the world I could go for three days and nights without food and water," he told me. "I went in there to get help."

I thought about it. The first three dances were the same when I went in. At my fourth Sun Dance, something pulled me, some urge. I said to myself, "I'm going to go down to the Sun Dance center pole." Ever since then, I've been all right. I quit counting how many times I've gone to the Sun Dance. Nowadays the Sun Dance is different. It seems they misinterpret the whole thing. Indian religion now has a modern touch to it; it's not tribal anymore. What was restricted is open. Still, it is very serious.

There are many ways you can Sun Dance. If a person is sick, he is not looking for a vision. A person who is there for his health already knows and is not seeking. People who have never had experience with the Sun Dance, young people, might seek a vision. What they want to do with it is another question. People with experience know that the Sun Dance is there to help you. Sometimes this vision quest turns into something else; I think that's why people stay away from it. If you go into a dance with an idea that you're going to see something, are you going to come out and say, "Well, I danced the Sun Dance," and use the experience in a different way? If so, you're going to come to a point where it will work against you. Most vision quest seekers are doing it for personal reasons, not to help people, but to talk about themselves in the way of having spiritual power. Most of the elders see it that way.

Let me give you a comparison. If you are in pain in the hospital, you need a shot of morphine to put your mind at ease. You feel better. That's the feeling you get from morphine, but as time goes on, the morphine wears off and the pain comes again. In a way, going into a Sun Dance could be like that. The pain there is not really pain, but it's your life, the way you went in there; you're at this stage. As time goes on, because of the absence of water and food, your body changes, your life changes.

When it changes you begin to feel different. All at once you begin to feel that same feeling the patient felt with morphine; you have no worries. You're in an area where you reach out and touch the Spirit with your mind; he's open to you. You can talk to him or whatever you want to do. When you get in that area, people say you can talk to God or you can talk to yourself. Both will be the same.

That feeling is what people call spiritual power, but to me and the other older ones, it's different. That is merely an opening to every part of your body, your life, your spirit. It's open to everything. That's all it is. There's nothing there that he's going to give you that you're going to use against anybody else, either healing people or using against people. Your spirit has power; you learn how to use that. Everything's going to be within you already.

Indian people attend not to look at the dancers but to experience a feeling; watching the dancers is part of it. I think people already know what they want out of the Sun Dance.

When you're dancing, your mind is supposed to be on only one thing: the center pole. You have a reason for going in there, a purpose; you don't just go in there to be dancing. You've got to pray; you've got to think; you've got to do it for someone. You've got to go for a reason; maybe somebody who needs help, that's why you're going. Maybe you're sacrificing your time for that person or a group of people; maybe you're doing it for a group of people who lost their relative. Or maybe you made a vow you would do this. Anyway, you go in for this certain reason; it's not a show.

Each song is sung one after another, on and on. You sleep and you hear the drums. It's constant. I've seen people dance, and they change. Their bodies change, their spirits change. You can actually see their expressions change. The song carries them. The ground is so hot, yet when these spirits and songs get ahold of you, you can dance over it without feeling the heat. You forget about hunger; that's a secondary thing in your mind. You're hungry the first day; the second day, you're different. The second day, the third day, you are just a body with a spirit, and you're not even thinking about food. You have made it; you have made it into another world.

In this world you drink coffee, you get hungry. It's habit. Just because it's morning, you get hungry; just because it's noon, you get hungry; evening time, the same way. The other world is not like that; it's different. The first day you Sun Dance, you get hungry. You're hungry at noon. Then, when the sun gets beyond that, you're not hungry any more. Supper time, you get hungry; beyond that hour, you aren't hungry any more.

In the night, they wake you before the sunrise. I get up early, about four o'clock. It's nice and clear. I walk around with a blanket. I think about a lot of things, about people, about my life. I smoke and pray.

Long before the dance, I will have cut red willow branches and peeled them; under the skin is a white substance. I scrape that off with a knife and dry it. I collect a certain amount and, when it's dry, I grind it really fine. Then I mix it with tobacco, a round leaf from a maple that grows in the mountains. I grind it all really fine. It makes a mixture with a sweet aroma or taste. When you smoke it, it gives you a moist feeling. It's an easy draw. I use that in the Sun Dance.

Early in the morning when the sun is coming up, you can take the first glimpse of that light, facing east, and pray for yourself or for people you know who need help. Pray at that time, and when the sun comes up, it hears your prayer. My uncles tell me the sun has a power like an arrow. You put an arrow in your bow and you shoot. The sun does the same thing; when it comes up, it shoots. That's what the Sun Dance ceremony is based on. The first ray of sunlight is like an X-ray; it goes right through your body, through your mind. You've got to stand there and absorb that.

When you first attend a Sun Dance, it's difficult because you can't adjust. Then one day you find yourself dancing and talking to the birds. You don't care if people watch. Let them watch. It's me. They came to see me and see the things that I feel. When you get that way, people recognize that.

56   I got acquainted with the Sun Dance. I became its friend and it became my friend—like the weather. When I go there, I know what I'm looking for. It is during a ten- or fifteen-minute span within the three days that the Spirit makes its visit with you—it's that brief. If you're playing around, sleeping, or outside, or too busy looking at people, you're going to miss it. It's a feeling of a different color. It's a separation from this life. You feel the world move.

One day I found myself sitting there, and the circle began to spin; it became spherical and began to spin, real slow. I could see ice; I could see countries; I could see clouds. I was seeing the Earth from another world.

I explained that to one of my relatives later on. He was an older person, a Sun Dancer, a medicine man. "That's as far as you go," he said. "That's as far as you go. No person can tell you otherwise because you were there. You saw it."

THE SUN DANCE

Neola, Utah

The Sun Dance Grounds are located in Neola, Utah, five miles northeast of Clifford Duncan's home.

APRIL 15, 1991

The Sun Dance Grounds, located in Neola, Utah, are five miles northeast of Clifford Duncan's home.

APRIL 15, 1991

Clifford Duncan at the Sun Dance Grounds in Neola, Utah.

APRIL 15, 1991

White Ways

Nowadays, I pray for my white friends the same as I pray for myself, the same as I pray for my mother. I have lived with white people in Salt Lake City and in the Uintah Basin enough to know that they have problems too; they get sick too; they cry too; they hurt too, just like we do. We get sick, we cry, we laugh, we die too.

As Native Americans, we pictured ourselves alone because we were separated from the white people, put aside on the reservation. If somebody would lock the doors on our home, for instance, when just the family was there, after so many years we would begin to consider only ourselves: "Somebody locked the door—God help us." In that situation I would not pray for the outside world because it would not be my concern. But when you really look at the outside, you find it's no different than what you know that's within.

The mind has a lot to do with how you accept the world. Whether you are in the city, or the country, or traveling, your mind can get ahead of you. You can walk yourself through a situation while sitting in one place, in the same way that a person lying down is already standing. I'm already at my destination, then I flash back and I'm here again. What I've seen in my life makes that possible. But if you live in one place, you have no way of projecting that. How does a person who lives on the same reservation all his life have any idea of what is on the outside? How does he know how to behave if he has never seen life anywhere else?

My people, the young ones, they started back in the 1930s and 1940s to accept the view of the white people. You listen to schoolteachers; you listen to white people; you listen to others. They're talking about evolution. Indian people want to hear these things, and they accept it. But they go so far in this world, so many decades, that when somebody else talks about Indian ways, they say, "No, that's your way."

Assimilation takes place in a short period of time. Then people want to go back and learn Indian ways, but it's too late. I think Indian ways should be taught to children when they're young, up to the age of about seven, or ten. Then they know what is there. By being taught, I mean this: take them to ceremonies; leave them with Indian families, especially the elders; let them eat Indian food so when they grow up they will know what it is. But Indian people somehow don't do that.

Say, you bring a child in. She's twelve years old. You put cooked rabbit in front of her. She says, "Yuck, what's this? I don't want to eat it. Have you got any bologna?"

If you have a child who's been around it, they'll say, "Yeah, that's good. I like it. Cook some more of that."

That's the thing we're looking at now. Too many of the people are that way. Then if someone else tries to teach their child Indian ways, they'll say, "Don't do that to my child. I can teach them." But they don't.

It's simple to pick up white ways. I can buy a car, drive. I can dress like a white person, talk like a white person. But there's another part to it, and that's where we get it wrong. The white people know where they came from. The Indian people know, too, where they came from, but they live in a different world. So that's where they bounce back. Later, I find Europeans are different from Americans, yet that's where Americans come from—that's the Old Country. Indians don't have an Old Country, because it's here. We've always been here.

12

City Living

In 1956 or 1957, after I married, I lived in Salt Lake City. I met my wife for the second time when she moved back to Randlett, on the Uintah-Ouray Reservation.

In a way, we were brought up in different worlds. I had known her in high school, but she transferred to an Indian high school in Phoenix, Arizona. Later she graduated from an Indian nursing training program in Laughton, Oklahoma, then worked in a hospital in Crownpoint, New Mexico. During that time she had a boyfriend who was a white doctor.

We got married a short time after she returned to the reservation, and then we moved to Salt Lake City. It may have been mostly her idea to move there. She had a job as a nurse at the LDS Hospital. I looked for work as a laborer.

There was a feeling, a city feeling, that I cannot describe. As one experiences it when one first goes to the city, it's like half-numbness. The people are half numb. They radiate the same feeling that you radiate, but it numbs out before it reaches you. Everybody is working in a system; everybody works on time.

You stand on the corner and wait for the bus. The bus comes along. You throw in a dime and walk back, sit down. You find that this bus is not for you, it's for somebody else. Also, they don't say, "Hey, Clifford—it's your corner. Get off." It's up to you to say, "I missed it," and get off at the next corner. Maybe you didn't pull the string right. Nobody does anything for you, but they watch you. The only thing they say is this: "You were supposed to get off at the last stop." So you experience that. And you go on and on and on.

Life is so fast, too. You are looking for work, and you're looking for a place to stay; you're looking for the right places to go. So all of this is working on you. You're actually getting away from everybody, to prove to your parents and yourself that you can live on your own. What sounds good on the reservation doesn't turn out that way in the city. It's so easy to say, "Well, you'll find a place to live. Why don't you stay here a day and look for a place." It's a frustrating experience.

Certain people say that you spend the younger part of your life forming a habit or making a mold for yourself to fit into—that's you. Then later in life, you find that those same people say the habit you built controls you; you have a bad habit. You're going to have a hard time getting away from the habit that you so busily put together in your younger days. Well, I say that the mold actually is patterned after how other people live.

Coming from high school into the world, you dress like them; you have a haircut; you pick up a fashion magazine and you buy the same clothes. You have a desire to buy a car, too, a fast car; everybody talks about a Cadillac, so you want a Cadillac too. Everybody talks about being a certain way: you've got to be intelligent; you've got to understand how to listen to classical music; you've got to know something about Shakespeare. So you try to follow along just to be like the others. Eventually you find that when you follow, that's not really you.

I make a mold and I fit into that and move to Salt Lake City. There I will refine myself so when I come back to the reservation people can tell a difference between the refined person and the former one. I resolve to live like them; I look for a job and I work; I buy a car; I have certain tastes; I've got to buy this and that. Then I go back to the reservation for a short period of time and people look at me and say, "Oh, you live in the city."

I talk about the city life, but only about the good things I experience. All the bad things, I don't want to talk about. I don't want them to say, "Well, it's no good." But I know it's no good, too.

After high school, I felt that everything was on me—I was going to have to succeed by myself. And I knew one thing: I would never receive a diploma for that. I wanted to show myself I could do some things, that I could learn. I wanted to be different, to get ahead. I wanted to understand the world in a different way; that was part of it, too. I wanted to be a person somewhat ahead of my time; that was the main thing. I wanted to be a person ahead of my time.

Maybe wanting this was a crutch—if I can't be any other thing, maybe my mind can be the big person in my life. Then, too, Indian people may tend to stay at one level because they have a communal type of life. I wanted to get ahead of that, yet at the same time be part of it. I think that was the most important thing in my life at that time: how to be ahead of myself and talk about different things. Then when I went home, people would say, "We don't know what you're talking about. We don't do it that way." Later, I believed, they would do it the way I said. I think that desire is what drove me.

I did learn, too. I learned how people live. I got acquainted with people at almost every level. I would study how they lived, how they talked, how they acted, why they acted that way. Salt Lake City was my classroom.

I met some new friends. A young Navajo man was an unusual friend to me. When I was first there, I didn't have a car. He had a brand new car, this young man. One day he said, "I can get to my work quicker than you because I live near my job. Why don't you drive my car? Drive it around as long as you want."

That's what he said. So I did. He was making payments, all of that, and I was driving it around, going to meetings on the reservation. Later he worked in Dugway. After I moved back to the reservation, his wife called me one day and said, "I wanted to tell you your friend died." He had died several months earlier of a rare illness that was job-related—something in his blood. I said goodbye to my friend.

While I lived in the city I used to go to the library, located on State Street where the Hansen Planetarium was located. It was really a cozy little library then. I had a library card, too; I learned how to use it.

I used to go upstairs and check out these books called the *Bureau of Ethnology Reports*. At first I didn't know what "ethnology" meant, but I knew the books must contain something old. After looking, I knew "ethnology" meant studies of a group of people, different groups. I'd go to the oldest book. They were reference books, the type you don't take out. So I would take my drawing pads to the library with me and go through the books page by page, sketching. I'd look at the photographs, the drawings, read about certain tribes, how they'd fix certain things, their designs. Next page, read that, on and on. One sketch called "Home of the Deities" was a very old design. That thing stuck in my mind a long time, and I tried to picture it in a different way.

Art had a lot to do with my habit of studying these books. My father did paintings once in a while on canvas; then he would give them away or someone would buy them. My other brothers did some paintings. One of my brothers was very good at beadwork, the best beadwork I've seen yet. He didn't do any paintings, he didn't do any sketches; but when you'd sit him down with beads he'd sketch out designs. My dad made paintings once in a while. He was busy all the time, and he couldn't spend a lot of time painting. I think he was interested in it, and if he'd had the time and money I think he would have gone into that, too. He was a self-taught person.

He talked about Indian art, the two-dimensional type. He would say, "This is Indian art; now this is realistic art. This is an Indian painting." The Indian paintings he showed me were almost like pictographs—symbolic not realistic—odd-shaped horses, bears like those on teepees during Custer's time. That was Indian art to him. He would discuss the difference, such as using solid colors—flat colors with no shading. When I did my sketches, I would look for those techniques in my own work and try to study what he was talking about.

I remembered how, when I went to school in Fort Duchesne, my teacher asked me to draw Indian designs on watch fobs for veterans in the hospital. She wanted me to do that, but I couldn't really understand what an Indian design was to her—what she wanted. I asked myself, what is an Indian design? I didn't know. After thinking about it, I realized she was talking about geometric beadwork designs like moccasin designs. That's what she was talking about; but she would ask for Indian symbols. That stuck with me—the way she said that and me trying to follow her directions.

After high school, I did quite a bit of painting. Once I got out of the service, I would do several paintings at a time, maybe six, seven. It would all depend on how I felt, how far I could go with it. Then when I put it away, I put it away. In spurts it would come back. I'd paint again and put it away again. You have to enjoy doing it; your body's got to be in it, your spirit's got to be in it.

For some time then, I'd tried to clarify within myself what I thought Indian art was. That's when I decided to look into old books in the library and began studying the ethnology books, compiled from reports sent in each year from every agency.

Also I saw collected newsletters called "Indians at Work," with stories about different Indians who drove tractors or caterpillars, doing engineering work. The newsletter was based on assimilating Indians into mainstream America. The newsletters featured Indian artists, too, and they talked about Indian art. I read those articles, trying to figure out my question: what is Indian design? Then I learned to categorize art based on the type of Indians. Southwestern Indians did art differently than plateau people; plains people were different from woodland people. I began to ask, how did my people create art? What was there for us? That's when I began going methodically through the books, starting with the earliest.

For a long period of time during and after high school, I had wanted to get away from learning. To hell with them, I thought; I wanted to go to Haskell and they said no. When I went to Salt Lake City, however, one thing I had in mind was this: if I can get training under the GI Bill, I will do that. They are going to pay my way. So I studied electronics at a place called the Radio Institute, just beyond Broadway, upstairs. We studied by categories, first an introduction—a lot of theory, reading about atoms. I learned how protons and neutrons work, how an atom contains them, and how you measure the separation. You use instruments like oscilloscopes or meters that measure ohms, amps. By collecting registers from certain ohms, you can track down whatever goes in there.

I learned how sounds amplify and what circuit that takes. I found that the radio has different circuits, so I studied all of that. I learned to deal with numbers I had never experienced in life, such as tangents, co-tangents, signs, co-signs, and learned how they work with angles. This really interested me as I began to understand something I had always wondered about—how does the radio work? As a child, I used to look inside the radio my dad had in the 1940s, searching for the people talking inside that thing. "They're not in there, but they're talking and my dad listens to it."

This class opened a door. I studied for several months, then moved to radio transmitters, receivers, and their operation. I could look at a schematic and figure out how the whole thing went together. I learned a little bit about that and received my third-class operator's license. I was ready for my second-class license, but I never did go back and apply. The third-class license was enough for broadcasting even in a radio station. Eventually I quit. I think I got a job someplace else. Maybe I got burned out, too, I don't know. But I worked; I worked.

I worked as an orderly in the psychiatric ward at LDS Hospital and, for a short time, in the gerontology ward. While working in the gerontology ward, I began doing the same thing I had questioned in others. As an observer, I couldn't understand the way they treated the old people. Then I found out that something about the things that happen in a hospital makes you become disgusted. You change a diaper and they turn around and dirty it in a few seconds. You ask, why didn't they do that in the other one?

When you're taking care of children, especially your own, you're not looking at the diaper; you're thinking how much you love your kids. Love has something to do with turning that a little to the side so it doesn't seem the way it did with an old person.

Around that time I got friendly with some white people, a white boy and his father, who was an assistant professor at the university and worked with Indian programs. When they first started Indian groups, they had a small church and would have meetings with six or seven families. That's where I met these white fellows. Sometimes I would visit and stay overnight. They used to put on dances for show, not as ceremony. They would put on programs in different schools, and people would come and watch. The Indians were mostly Navajo, some Pueblo. They had been in Salt Lake for quite a while and were Mormons. I was the only Ute, but I did the war dance for them.

We had our first child in Salt Lake City, and so a lot of my female cousins would come out and stay with us and babysit. At first we lived on Seventh East before it was widened, and later we lived in the Avenues on "B" Street. During those years I kept in touch with my religion and would go back to the reservation for meetings. Sometimes, in wintertime especially, I would take the bus from Salt Lake City to Roosevelt, then get a ride up to Whiterocks. My wife worked different schedules, evening shift, graveyard shift, so we really didn't make plans in advance because her schedule changed.

Once during the summer after I attended a meeting, I sat on a bus going home. I was watching out the window—watching the heat waves ripple and rise. Out in a flat area I saw some people coming, walking, big people, so big they seemed magnified. I watched them and thought maybe I was imagining them, but they were so real. What made them different was that they went in and out of this heat wave.

Finally they went in and disappeared. I often went back to that place, but only the heat wave was there.

Later I bought a car and would drive out to meetings. I was something of a good man because I took care of my baby. I would give her baths, change her clothes, fix her formula. When I wanted to go to a meeting, we would get in the car and together we would come out, the baby and me. Every so often I would stop and change her diaper, feed her. When I reached Whiterocks, I would leave her with somebody and go to the meeting, then pick her up and drive back. I learned about babies and how to take care of them. That was an experience by itself, on-the-job training.

My wife understood Indian ways differently than I did. Her way was that you go to the hospital when you get sick. The doctor is the one who will fix a sick person, prescribe whatever medication you need, do an operation, and that's the way it is. She was trained that way.

Then, on the other side, I would say no, "I have this Indian medicine that works in a spiritual way. I'm going to pray for our child and she is going to get well." Or I would say, "I'm going to give her sagebrush tea," or "I'm going to fan her with an eagle feather."

"No, that's not going to work. We have to take her to the hospital."

If our child was sick with strep throat, I would say, "I'm going to doctor her with a throat swab."

"No, you might damage her throat. You can't do that."

"Well, let's try. Our people have been doing that for years and years and years. It breaks the fever. We know how to do that."

"No, you can't do that because it's not sanitary."

So we would have these little fights, who's right, who's wrong. I would go to my meetings on the reservation, and she would say, "I've got to go to work."

I would think, "Well, she doesn't believe my way. I don't believe her way either."

13

Peyote Meetings

From time to time, my elders would relate to me information about a man named Sam Lonebear, who was working with the Uintah Railway to bring rail service to Vernal from Grand Junction. At the same time, Lonebear had some experience with traveling because he had worked for Wild West shows. Among other things, he picked up sleight-of-hand tricks from other performers.

However, Lonebear actually reached our reservation after studying something far more serious in Oklahoma—the rituals associated with peyote ceremonies. So with those ideas, he came on to the Uintah-Ouray Reservation and began to teach the people here. He started with a sick person who needed help because he had not received much relief from his medical doctor. Now, the doctor seemed to be giving up on him. By using peyote, Lonebear helped to get this person well. So that's how peyote was established on this reservation—the peyote healed.

With that explanation, you get an idea what type of people were likely to accept peyote, and how peyote is then introduced to different groups. Peyote is central to all things within that ceremony. It is sometimes described as being a motivator; I would have to say that people can be like that, too. People can influence you to do things or to feel a certain way. If the leader is one way, everybody's that way. If the leader one day changes his mind and says, "Let's do away with communal thinking. Let's have a different way of life," everybody may change. In Europe, for instance, people are turning away from the old systems they have followed for so many decades. We have seen that happen. It did not necessarily happen with a change of leadership; it happened within the same leadership. Peyote has the power to do that, too.

Recreational use is not part of peyote's real purpose. It makes me feel bad to realize that there are a lot of people who want to do things wrong, even intelligent people. You take attorneys; certain ones are disgusting. They're disgusting in the way they can twist your words around to change the meaning to exactly the opposite of what you are saying. Then they'll say, "Just answer me, yes or no." Yes or no does not always answer a question. But they'll take that and say, "You said no." And so change occurs.

Human nature is sometimes like that. That's why people have so many problems. We have so many problems *we* have created—laws that benefit a few people but have a tendency to hurt others. Eventually it comes to the point where all the politicians are going to work against each other, and that's the end of the world. Why can't people go back to the simple way of life? If something belongs to me, fine; it doesn't belong to you. If it belongs to you, it doesn't belong to me.

Everyone knew when automobiles were first manufactured that the engines used oil and gas; everyone knew that would eventually pollute the air. But they didn't want to say that because, over here, is a man who sells gas. He says, "Well, I'm making money. I'll give you money if you'll take care of me, speak for me."

At the time, the Indian people said, "That's wrong."

And the dominant society replied, "You're backward. This is progress." Now some will admit we're destroying our world. So who was right? But still, most politicians and industrialists don't want to admit it.

They do things according to the law or according to how they can benefit. For some time now, a case regarding peyote has been traveling the judicial system. The central issue of being Indian is within that controversy; it is part of the language, part of the ceremonial ways. If you take peyote out, you're bothering the rest of the ritual, too.

Eventually they say, "Well, you're losing your culture; let's put it all back together."

Too late. So why do they adopt harmful practices in the first place and then object to the results? They say, "If I say that, it's going to be that way."

Why not let me be the one to decide? If a white person lobbies for a law, it will be so. If an Indian speaks up, many will say, "He doesn't have a degree. He doesn't understand it."

Christopher Columbus did not come here to discover America; he came here because he was looking for gold. Out of that venture came destruction, too. The Europeans destroyed the Indian way of life. Ironically, if you look at the history of some of European countries—Spain, for instance—what they brought from the jungles of South America destroyed them, too. Spain had a lot of power at the time of Columbus, but Spain has lost that power. The trading routes they used coming around Africa, all that rich area they used to have was destroyed, because they began getting their silver from someplace else. When there is more silver than gold, the economy shifts.

If white people really want to do something about the world, if they truly regard the world as the center of life, the first thing they have to do is learn to love the world; then they would know how to take care of it. But the way they've been operating is, "I'm for you, and you're for me. You pat my back, I'll pat yours." Then it goes so far, and unexpected things come in.

It was easy for drugs to come into our society because of unemployment. Morale was so low that drugs could run rampant through the whole world without stopping for anything. It was so easy for anything to come in because of the problems we created ourselves. That's what I think.

It's easy to tear down a mountain, but it's hard to put it back the way it was. It's easy to tear apart feelings, but it's hard to put them back together the way they were before.

74

Whenever I went to a ceremony as a young man, or whenever I go now, it is always with the accepted knowledge that whatever I do will be motivated from within me, not from that particular ceremony but from life. When you get up in the morning, you know you've got to clean up, comb your hair, all of that. In going to meetings you go with the idea that you will eat medicine, you will smoke tobacco, you will use cedar, you will use sage, you will drink water, you will sing, you will listen to the drum, you will listen to people talk. You know what they're going to say; it's a matter of why they will say it in each particular meeting. So you already know in your mind why you are going.

Now if you went to a meeting and somebody said, "We're not going to eat peyote at this meeting," right away you would say, "Why not?" The meeting is like a puzzle. In order to create a complete picture you can enjoy, every piece must fit into it. Then you can see the picture. For my people, peyote would be that one piece to make the picture complete. The other elements, such as drums, gourds, and songs, are the same way. If they started the meeting with a different song, I would say, "Hey, that's not the right song. You've got to have a certain song at the beginning, as people did hundreds of years ago."

When the peyote is passed around, you don't think, "Well, I'll take five spoonsful so I can feel high." That thought is away from you totally. Your first thought is this: "Teach me something good." You sense that the peyote is God's; it belongs to someone superior to you. If you abuse it, you are wrong. You don't belong there—and you will *know* that by a feeling that you do not fit. When you take the peyote, your feeling is already moving with the ceremony. Already you are saying, "This has a sincere purpose behind it, the sincerity of these people." You can feel that, just as you can if you walk into the midst of people who are mourning or people celebrating a birthday. Your senses have a lot to do with how you accept things.

In the religious sense, peyote is one of the few ways left to Indian people, a door we can open ourselves and enter. When you take peyote, you do not expect to sit there and hallucinate; that's got to be far from your mind. The people who use peyote and are strong believers

have never had hallucinations. They never have seen one! They marvel at those who come in for the first time and say something like, "I saw this in beautiful colors; I saw a bird."

The Indian people are thinking, "God, what's this?"

Something was behind that experience for that person. Ceremonies and religious activities expose an inner feeling of an individual. If something happens to you in a ceremony, it was not the ceremony that caused it. The ceremony merely brought to the surface something already within you.

As a child, I was a sickly person, kind of meek. My brothers near my age were strong. They're both gone now. My cousins were strong, too; they're gone also. Sometimes I ask, "Why am I the only one left?" I tried to figure that out as time went on, and I finally realized that I had to focus on problems and resolve issues that they couldn't handle. In leaving this world, they put their load on my shoulders.

Several weeks after one brother's death, I went to a peyote meeting and I could feel that burden. That's when I mentally told my brothers, "That's why you left all of this load on me," and chuckled.

I went to the place my brother was buried and told him, "I know why you did this. Since I am living, I think it is best that I make up my mind to carry this load." That's what I said, and the same thing with my other brother. So I began to carry their load as far as I could, until their children grew up and were on their own. I didn't have to discipline their children, but I had to care for them—to carry them in the way of the Sun Dance beliefs. I had to talk to the children. Now they have children, and at certain times I need to be present for ceremonies for my nieces and nephews and their families, thus to pray for them.

Modern Living on the Reservation

After six years or so, I really didn't like the city; it wasn't what I wanted in my life. I wanted to get away from the constant rush, the constant movement of people. The rush was all for nothing because it never slowed down.

I think living in the city did make me aware of how people live on the other side and how they talk about this side—the Indian way of life. At the same time, one of the things I didn't like was that when you get bored—locked into a boring life that slowed you down—you have a tendency to walk down to the bar and start drinking. So eventually the only way you can get away from that is to walk away from it completely. That's what I saw there, with people.

In the city, you learn how people talk; you learn what they talk about. After so long, you begin to talk like they do. You begin to use their words because you want to be part of the group, and so you learn their words in order to carry on a conversation. It's the same with Indians and the way we talk. You can even break this down into professions. If you want to talk like a lawyer, you live with a lawyer. Eventually you learn to use their words.

Someone once said that language can change through watching television. You watch the news broadcasters, pay attention to how they talk, and you learn their technique. They're trained to speak that way. You teach yourself by watching television; you're not listening to the news but are watching the newscaster. As the world changes, you have to go along with change; you have to learn to accept change. You center your control not on people but on how to adapt. I see television as the great assimilator because it brings English inside the house rather than leaving it at school. My children, for instance, understand Ute but don't speak it.

I look at it this way: I have learned to think like any white person. I don't necessarily have to be intelligent in any other way but this—I think just like you. People say to be educated, you have to be able to communicate. That's good, that's important. Then you've got to learn *more* than what you already know; you've got to improve your vocabulary. I find that is only an instrument. I can express myself to almost anyone in the language I know how to use; and I can think like you. I may not talk like someone using complicated jargon, but I can think like you. I can understand the jargon, too, because I read. I listen to people talk.

If you learn the way I learned, you have to fake it at certain times. Education is like a road with holes in it, but you're going so fast you jump over the holes. I know certain things, but I find other people know more; so I have to agree with them or disagree. In reality, I may not know anything about a certain topic; but that gives me the opportunity to go back and study again.

Over the years, I had children, four girls and one boy. The children went to school in Whiterocks and Neola. Their life was a modern type of living: running water, electricity, telephone. They had transportation, everybody had transportation. You go to town whenever you need to. In my childhood experience, the Whiterocks store was the center for that community. There, you could buy almost everything you needed. Later, that changed; people would say, "If they don't have it in Whiterocks, let's go to Roosevelt. Roosevelt is a bigger town."

Some people were even going into Salt Lake City, as they do today. If I want to buy something, I would rather go to Salt Lake because I can find the type of product I want at lower cost. During the period when the dividend money was coming in for tribal members, people shopped in Roosevelt. The non-Indian people in Roosevelt took advantage of the situation. If a white person was in a store and wanted to buy something valued at fifteen dollars, the storekeeper would sell it for fifteen dollars. But when the Indian person walked in, they'd turn the tag over and it would be twenty-five dollars for the same thing. We came into Roosevelt and spent our money.

In returning to Whiterocks, I fit back in easily. It used to be that when Indian people spent several years away from the reservation, that made them superior in the community's way of thinking. That was the old idea back around 1910, 1920, 1930, when people were told that their religion was pagan or old-fashioned. "If you do that, you're backward. If you use an Indian language, you're backward. You've got to be dressed in updated fashion; you've got to have a necktie and wear a suit." A lot of Indian people believed that, and they went in that direction. When they worked in an office with a white person, they'd get a pat on the back congratulating the appearance of assimilation. Many people would leave their religion and join the Episcopal Church or the Mormon Church or whatever. So they would become part of the mainstream. Other Indian people accepted assimilation, but their hearts were still back here.

The old idea of assimilation later changed because people began to find that it doesn't work that way. Today you find certain families that have stuck with assimilation, this old idea that we're Indians living in a white world, so if we live like them, dress like them, go to school, have a degree, fine—then we're like them. On the other hand, it's important to consider the way you feel. You can do the same things without being tied into white society.

That's another way of looking at it. You can be a peyote person, you can be a Sun Dance person, you can be anything in this world that's Indian, yet have a college degree, too. That's another way of life, and I think that would be a better world than assimilation; but we haven't seen too much of that yet. People go to school to get an education and, right away, they change. They want to be accepted totally into white society.

Not too long ago, my cousin asked me to take his daughter into a sweat lodge before she went away to college. I told her it could give her the beginning of discipline. The sweat is a disciplinary instrument. God is there, everywhere; you have to understand him, and have that burning desire to learn, and to become whatever you truly want to be.

CLIFFORD DUNCAN AT HOME

Clifford Duncan in front of his childhood home in Whiterocks, Utah. His home burned down in the late 1990s.

APRIL 15, 1991

The back of Clifford Duncan's home in Neola, Utah.

NOVEMBER 25, 2016

Lodge poles by Clifford Duncan's home in Neola, Utah.

NOVEMBER 25, 2016

A shed in the back of Clifford Duncan's home in Neola, Utah.

NOVEMBER 25, 2016

Clifford Duncan with his quarter horses in the pasture behind his home in Neola, Utah.

APRIL 15, 1991

Clifford Duncan at home, working on his porcupine hair roach with a grouse feather visor for the
Ute Intertribal Powwow, Fort Duchesne, Utah.

JULY 8, 1990

Clifford Duncan examining an artifact found above Lapoint, Utah.

APRIL 15, 1991

Clifford Duncan near his childhood home in Whiterocks, Utah.

APRIL 15, 1991

Clifford Duncan next to his teepee at the Powwow Grounds.
Fourth of July Ute Powwow, Fort Duchesne, Utah.

JULY 7, 2008

Clifford Duncan next to his yellow pickup truck at the Powwow Grounds.
Fourth of July Ute Powwow, Fort Duchesne, Utah.

JULY 7, 2008

Clifford Duncan by his sweat lodge behind his home in Neola, Utah.

APRIL 15, 1991

Clifford Duncan at home in Neola, Utah.

JULY 1, 2012

Kennedy Years,
Johnson Inauguration

After settling again on the reservation, I worked with a boundary survey group. I worked with a young white fellow, a student of Brigham Young University. He was the instrument man, and I was the rodman; he would keep notes of the calculations.

We got to be good friends. At times, he would say, "Let me show you how to run this." "Let me show you how to calculate notes." "Let me show you how to use the right formula." So I would listen, and he would explain his techniques. I learned by actually applying his instructions as I heard them. I worked quite a while for that fellow.

I remember one day, late in 1963, it was snowing. I was working with a group of Indian men doing a survey, going over the boundary of the reservation and placing steel markers. That year we worked late into the fall, knowing that when the snow got deep, we would quit. This particular day it was cold. We were way out in the mountains.

After 4:30 we were driving back through the wooded mountains looking for deer. If we happened to spot one, we would take it and throw it in the back of the truck. We had our rifles with us; it was hunting season on the reservation. When we got to a place called Bear Wallow, we saw a raptor sitting on a burned pine tree, a stump with a single branch. We stopped the truck. The fellows said, "Well, maybe we'd better take that." Our idea was to use it during ceremonies.

So they shot it. The funny thing about it was that both guns fired at exactly the same moment. The bird fell, and we didn't know which fellow hit it. One of my brothers picked it up and brought it back. It was still alive so they killed it. We threw it in the back and drove home.

It was snowing as we drove back. When we got to Fort Duchesne, everything was quiet, almost silent. We knew that something had happened; something had gone wrong. As we parked the truck, some people came out and told us, "The president of the United States got shot; he was killed."

Later, we separated the bird; one took the wing parts, the tail; we divided it; each feather was given to a different one. One of the bones was given to me by my brother, the joint to the wing. That's what is used to make a whistle for the Sun Dance. Later, he fixed it, then gave it back to me again. When I went to Sun Dance, I used that. The other parts of the bird—I don't know what happened to them because all the people who were with me are gone now. They've died since that time. The bird bone whistle that was given to me, I still use today. I loan the extra whistles I have to people who ask, but I do not give that one to anyone.

John F. Kennedy's death saddened the Indian people. Prior to his assassination, the federal government seemed to be doing its work according to promises of the federal government. When the president of the United States has a sympathetic feeling for the Indians, the programs reflect that—they'll do something for the Indian. This is true of other parts of the government. During those times, it is easier for Indian people on the reservation to get along with white people. A good leader makes a lot of difference. Kennedy's views differed from those of certain other presidents—Andrew Jackson, for instance.

Kennedy happened to favor the Indian more than any other person in that office, so people on the reservation felt deeply sad at his death. You would hear people say, "Somebody stopped it. Right when it was getting to the point where things were going to be better for the Indian, somebody stepped in and killed that person." Since that point, we still haven't seen too much improvement although we've had a lot of Indian programs.

During Kennedy's time people were beginning to recognize the Indians. More was going for Indians and other minorities. Some of the tribes that had been terminated began getting benefits back under Kennedy's programs, though some did not. In fact, it was then that the mixed-bloods, who had been terminated from the Ute tribe, began to look this way and to decide they were Indians too. That was a turning point.

Lyndon Baines Johnson served out Kennedy's term. And in 1965, the Northern Utes were called upon to be a part of his inauguration parade in Washington, DC. From all over the country Indians were invited to come, and I was fortunate to go with the Ute group. About fifteen of us went to Salt Lake City to board a plane there, but the weather was very bad. They changed our schedules around. We took a train to Grand Junction and flew east from Denver.

When we arrived in Washington, DC, they took us to several hotels where they had made reservations for the Indian people. They had a big gathering where all the Indians congregated for instructions—a big planning meeting. Friends met friends—and that was it, the beginning of the mess. Friends met friends and they went all over, one big party. Fifteen of us were supposed to be in the parade, and only three of us made it. We dressed in our traditional regalia and rode horses. Our twelve companions had disappeared—we didn't know where.

To get our horses, we went to a stable out of town in Virginia. A German fellow in charge of the stables brought the horses into one little area to "give us our choice." He wanted to instruct us on how to ride the horses. He said, "You get on from the left side." He said, "These are reins."

He got horses for Harvey and Juanita. They got on and rode around. He got one for me, the slowest of all the horses. He said, "Kick it. Hit it with a stick like this."

So after working with it, I got it to move. We rode around the arena. Then I asked him, "Sir, could I exchange my horse? I want a livelier one."

He said, "No, those horses are dangerous." I insisted, and so he said, "Okay, but I warned you."

I saddled up using an English saddle. You squeeze it with your knees, touch it with your feet, turn this way, that way.

He said, "Get used to that horse because it's going to be a lively one."

"All right." I got on, touched the horse a little bit, and it moved—a good horse.

He said, "All right, can you make it run?"

"Yeah, sure." We loped around, did a figure eight.

That's when he said, "You know about horses."

"Yes, all of us do. Remember, we're Indians."

He said, "Why am I giving instructions to you people?"

The next day we got those horses to the starting line, out in front of the Capitol building. Those in charge told us, "Start on the south side, go up Pennsylvania Avenue, and so forth."

We had fun. There were so many people along the parade route, even in the January cold. We had special instructions. They said, "If you wave to the president, wave with your open hand. Otherwise the Secret Service agents are going to shoot you. If you lift and wave your feathers, they're going to shoot first and ask questions later." So we waved with open palms.

While I was in Washington I went to the Indian area of the Smithsonian Institute. They had a lot of religious instruments, and a lot of peyote hanging there. Later, as a tribal planner, I went back several times for additional visits.

16

Father's Death

There is a story from the 1930s about an Indian man walking alone one very dark night. He decided to follow the railroad tracks and see how far he could get that night. He walked and he walked. The only way he could tell he was going somewhere was by sometimes touching the rail on the right or left side. He walked on the ties; he could feel the solidness of the track.

Then he noticed it wasn't solid underfoot any more, so he reached down and found there was no earth underneath the ties. There was empty space under the ties and the rails, so he knew he was on a bridge. He didn't know if it was a high bridge or a low bridge. So he continued to walk forward and went on and on and on. He heard a whistle, way behind him; a train was coming. He heard it again, getting closer. Then the engine's light began to get brighter and brighter and brighter. The train was coming; the track began to shake.

He didn't know what to do, so he decided to get under the railroad track and hold on until the train passed over. He swung underneath and held on to the ties, interlocking his fingers. He hung there for ten or fifteen minutes as the train roared above him. He noticed he was weakening and might lose his grip. He decided to pray. He started praying to God. Finally, he gave up and let go. As he fell, he yelled his last cry, the end of his life.

But when he dropped, he fell only ten to twelve inches. All that time he had been hanging about one foot from the ground. He picked himself up and said, "God, never mind that prayer." He went on his way.

When I had my father, my father could instruct me. When I got sick or my children got sick, my father would be there. My father died in Price, Utah, in 1969. He and one of my brothers were working in Colorado, and they wanted to come home. They didn't have money, so they hitchhiked and got as far as Price. All of a sudden, my father just fell over. They took him to the hospital, and he died. He was a diabetic. I don't think the doctors knew that, so they probably didn't know how to treat him. When he went into a coma, they probably thought he was another drunken Indian.

My father was a teacher, a teacher who had different moods. Rather than just be a father straight through, at times it seemed he didn't care; but deep down it may have been different. So I use him as a teacher. No matter how I put that, he was an important person to me. People talk about having an idol, some person you follow; maybe that's how I use him. I remember the things he talked about, his views, and I feel comfortable knowing I accomplished some things he wanted within the things that I want, too.

When he died, I was left to wonder who would help me now that my father was gone. I moped around for a while, then said, "It's got to be me."

I wish I had listened more to my dad. I've learned by trial and error. I've been tested many times, and I test myself. The conclusion I came to was that I would depend on my religion—whether I believed it and believed in what I was doing.

I look at it this way: if I am going to do something for someone, I will lead them wherever they want to go until I complete that. If the people who are with me don't understand, fine. If they don't understand now, they will understand later.

My people know I do these things. If a sick person comes to me and asks for help, I tell them yes. I have to stand on what I believe because it's me that has to go deep down. That matters more than any other person's way of thinking because I have to be true to myself.

There comes a time in your life where you have to do something the way you think you should. Some people are a little different; they will never change no matter how old they get. They will always think like a child.

Somewhere down the line someone will replace me. I have to find that someone, one of my nephews, one of my grandchildren. Then I'll say, "You take it." That's who I am going to pass my ways to. If not my son, it will be one of them.

17

Medicine Man

Whether I lived in Salt Lake City or on the Uintah-Ouray Reservation, I was thinking about helping people. I stayed with that; I didn't separate myself from ceremonies. When I went to the city, I didn't put that away. I put a lot of things away, but not that. When I returned, I had no adjustment to make to strengthen myself. I was still at the same level.

One afternoon soon after I returned to the reservation, a man brought his brother to me. This young man, in his twenties, was stretched out in the back of the car. His name was Robert Jack. Robert was a diabetic, and a doctor had told him he had only two days to live. They had taken him to his uncle, a Sun Dance chief and shaman, who looked at him and said, "I can't do anything for him. I'm sorry."

Robert's brother described all this to me.

I said, "He's going to die anyway, so he's got nothing to lose. If he wants to live, he'll make it."

I went over to the young man, bent close, and looked at him. I said, "I'm going to work on you, and you're going to live."

He whispered, "Yeah!"

We set up the teepee and cleaned up, getting ready. That night we took him into the teepee. I gave him a triple amount of peyote, maybe more. He crawled around, completely overpowered, while we talked and prayed. Then, at one point, he went stiff.

"I think we lost him," his brother said.

"Stand him up," I told them. They did, and he was still stiff. "Move every part of his body."

We continued praying, singing, and moving him for more than two hours. Then one of his arms began to move on its own, to the rhythm of the drum.

The next morning he was all right. I asked him what he had experienced during the service. He said, "I was gone. I slipped out. I moved through a tunnel that went way out there into space. I could hear a faint drumbeat. I came closer and could hear you guys singing. Then I slipped back, faster and faster, and came back to life." He is middle-aged now and has few health problems now and then.

In healing, the individual has to be half of it, the ceremony the rest. I was willing him to live, all the way through. I look at that experience this way: because I was a part of an ongoing ceremony, I was asked to play a certain role at a crucial time. This man asked me to do my part for the spiritual power to heal his brother. If I give a person medicine, it's the medicine that's going to heal, not me. If I talk to the Man That Made This World, I am asking him to help me help this person. That's what I'm doing. I'm part of the process, but I'm merely carrying it. I look at it that way. God's healing power was within him.

Yet I had worked for that experience. With spiritual power, you have to earn it. You have to submit your life; you can't buy it. Nobody can give it to you, and say, "here, you've got it now." You've got to work for that in order for whatever you're thinking to happen. It's going to fail sometimes, but most of the time it's going to work.

Maybe when you're young, you go into it this way: I'm going to have fun; it's going to be good; it's never going to go wrong. But as time goes on, you begin to find that it takes work. People die, too. Sometimes you're going to have a hard time. People are going to get sick. Sometimes you're going to walk away from it. You're going to say no. You will think, why did I ever do this? Why did I want to be this?

Then, eventually, you're going to be by yourself. All the people you used to depend on are going to die off and leave you by yourself. You have to understand that after you have picked up healing ways, and you have gone through a training process, deep down, you know you cannot quit. That is one requirement, that you do not quit. You've picked it up, and, no matter what, you can't give up. So, when they bring a sick person to you, you cannot say, "No, I cannot do it."

Then why did you do it that very first time? Why did you start that meeting? If you knew that someday you were going to refuse, you should have said, "I don't want to do that because someday some person is going to come to me in need and say, 'I want you to help me.'" If I was going to turn down that man later on, I should have never started it. That's how I look at it: you have to do it.

You may not know how to do it. There may be no way you could do it, but you have to think it out: How am I going to do this? Who is going to give me a description of the way it could be done? So you start thinking it out: Okay, I'm going to do it this way. I know that's going to work. You have to be positive. It's going to work because I learned it that way, and this person's going to think that way, too. She learned it the same way. You can't go into anything thinking it might not work, especially with a really sick person.

If you come to me and say, "I want you to help me," if I'm not ready at that time, I will say, "Well, I'll come back. We'll do it then." I have to think through the main core, then trim away the fringes—it's like trimming a hedge, for instance. You've got to take all that excess off, then once you see the core clearly, you're ready. My way of thinking is like that too, sometimes. It carries with it a lot of doubts, and a lot of ideas that might work or might not work. Somewhere is the way that it's really going to be.

If you come to me and say, "I want you to help me," I say, "Fine." I have to put away the idea that you are white and deal with you as a person. But I'm looking at you as a white person first. With an Indian, it's the same way if the person belongs to another tribe. I have to figure out what they believe in. I have to do it in a way that I don't disturb any of their beliefs.

So all of that went into this meeting they asked me to conduct for Robert. I had dealt with others first, but not serious illnesses, just colds or problems that you know they're going to get well from. Even today, though, I don't consider myself to be a person who has power to do things. But I do know other things have power. The Man That Made This World is number one, then he may have delegated a lot of power to other things, a lot of different spirits in this world. They're the ones that are doing it, and I have to call on them.

I've seen this, too. For instance, you and I are here together. If you ask me to help you, and I start out by saying, "I want you to help me," to this Supreme Being, I'm always doing that in my mind. Yet somewhere along the line I will have a tendency to forget that approach, and I will start talking to you. First, I will make the approach to the man who is superior to me, with the idea that I'm a pitiful person; I don't know anything. Then all at once, I change around, and here's the way it is.

Then you begin to wonder, "How come he's into another world now?" I've seen that happen. I think about that. I think it's best to maintain the position that you don't know too much when it comes to spiritual powers. If you elevate yourself, you're going to lose yourself. If you think you know more than you really know, you're going to get into trouble. I believe in that strongly. I think a human is only a human; but the quicker you accept the fact that you *don't* know all you know, the better you'll be. If you know so much, fine, you know it. If you don't know it, don't pretend. Say, "That's it; I don't know." If you don't know, you don't know.

This experience with Robert didn't have any particular impact on me, or the way people saw me. It was a world already made. It makes a happier life if you are only living for what's already going to be there for you. Your life is merely that—exposure to something that's already there.

Also the people around here knew me when I was a little boy. Somehow when you're around people, you remember how they were as a child, and that's always going to be there. Whatever they do after they're grown up reflects on what they did when they were young.

People are going to look at it from that point of view, and recent things are going to be new. If your children do something today, you say, "Well, they were like that when they were little." On the other hand, there is something new, also. There will be two things you see—the old and the new—all the time, the young and the older person.

If all at once someone in your family says, "Hey, I'm a medicine man," the first thing that comes to your mind is, "I've got to laugh at this." Then maybe if they start doing something spiritual, you say, "Well, maybe they're right," and then you begin to change. If we start talking about medicine ways, someone will say, "Well, he's not really like that." And it's true because they're looking at it their way. But someone else will say, "He is a medicine man because he helped me through that trouble," or, "When we were together he did this." And that's true, too. I guess it's a matter of how you carry yourself from there to here.

I accept the white man's way of doing things. I have studied medical ways, read about them. Doctors do an operation: your body works this way; it's like your heart pumps oil and gas into your system. I accept that. If your kidneys go out of whack, if your liver is all beat up, you've got to do away with certain parts and get spare ones.

But I also believe this, and it is beyond myself. If one only knows how, one can make a sick person well in a split second. I believe that way. I believe one can dissolve a virus, if one knows how, through spiritual ceremonies. But it has to be this way: if you want help, you must tell me ahead of time. It's going to be my individual project to bring myself to the point where I'm ready. Before certain ceremonies, I am going to talk to my Creator about everything in my life. At certain points, I am going to break down and cry. He already knows what I'm going to say, but I go through it anyway. When I have brought myself to a certain level, then I will tell you, "I'm ready."

Then I don't want anyone to bother me. I don't want to talk to anybody. When I approach that ceremony, I need to have a strong feeling that it's going to work. Then I will try to help. The weaker you are, the stronger I have to make myself. If I know that you are strong, you can do it on your own, but I will lead you to the door. You can open the door and go in. If you're not strong enough, I will open the door, walk in with you, and lead you out.

Indian people understand this; they accept it; this healing does exist. But most won't talk about it for fear of saying something wrong, or being brainwashed by others who don't understand.

A LONE TEEPEE

Neola, Utah

Clifford Duncan at his home in Neola, Utah.

JULY 7, 1992

Clifford Duncan setting up a teepee at his home in Neola, Utah.

JULY 7, 1992

Divorce and Remarriage

In the mid-1970s, I went through a major change in my personal life. You can learn from others or, if you don't want to listen to people, you can learn the hard way. I think it sticks when you learn it yourself.

When I was young, I would hear people talking: "Well, they're not living in the right way." They talked about always showing the best side of yourself, about taking care of your family, providing for your family, working hard so you'll have a good family. They said, "Don't go out and bother people." They talked about that, too. They said a husband shouldn't leave his wife for another woman, or a woman leave her husband. They talked about not growing up to rely on alcohol. That was stressed, too.

As I grew up, I found that Indian people were not really the way we were told to be. It was a common thing for a man to leave his family and pick up another woman, and for the woman to find another man. There were a lot of people doing that. But I thought, I'm not going to be that way. I'm going to be a good man; that's bad. I still remembered how they talked about that.

Still, in my teenage years I started going with different young women and lived with one really young lady before I turned twenty. My mother and father didn't say anything about it. I had other girlfriends, too, and brought them around the house. And they didn't say anything about that, but I knew it was wrong. It bothers me today that I did those things in front of my mother and father.

Years later I got married legally and we had four children. I lived with my wife sixteen years, then I broke away from her. We separated, got divorced. Then I remarried, but my second wife had been married, and had children. I broke up that family, too. She was younger than I, about seventeen years difference. We have been married for nineteen years.

My wife's aunt and her husband raised her from the time she was a child. When she was divorced and staying with them, I went to their house and they said, "Don't let that man in." Later I went to their home after we were married, and her uncle gave me a lecture about almost nothing. He stood in the middle of the room talking, talking, talking. To this day I still feel it: her people don't accept me. But I talk to them. I do things for them. I'm not asking them to forgive me. I'm not asking them to pay me. I still pay for what I did. They're strong Episcopalians.

When I lost my wife and family, everything else I had went too. One day I was standing there with nothing but what I had on. The judge who handled our case was my ex-wife's sister, a tribal judge. When I was standing before her, she stripped me of everything. What could I say? She said, "You will give everything to her. You will pay for this, this. You will sell your pickup and give the money to the children. The car is going to belong to her. Everything in the house goes to her, too."

That's it. You can't fight tribal court. Then I started over from the bottom. I told myself I still had time; in ten years I would have it all back. Well, things were all right up to a certain point, and then I began to feel guilty—I had done something wrong. The feeling would go away then come back again. I finally accepted the whole situation. I have to live my life this way because I caused those things to happen. I'm going to have to pay for that. I knew it was wrong to split up a family, and I blame myself for that.

I also live with this, too. I am going to be old before too long. When you get old your body changes. I'm going to get sick; I don't know what kind of a sickness I'm going to catch, but that's going to be mine. My wife will still be a young lady, and she's going to marry somebody else. I know that. I have to accept these things. When you live in my world, it's a world mixed with guilt and also with acceptance of how you're going to end up—it's going to be the way you're thinking.

When I see any of our grown children having problems related to the absence of a parent in their early years, I try to step in. Sometimes I can't handle the several areas at once. If I spend too much time with one side, my wife says something about it: "You're spending too much time with your other kids." These problems exist; this is the life situation of the majority of Indian people because that's how we live.

Nowadays, it's worse because both the man and the woman work. Back when Kennedy came up with the Community Action Programs, they started talking about providing training and employment for both husband and wife. They got the wives out of the homes and put them out in front in restaurants, in offices. Along with that came problems that would arise in families. There were a lot of divorces, separations, fights, different lifestyles. After every work week, people would go to a bar and have a party to relax. Before that people didn't talk about having a party at somebody's house or at the bar. But now you go into an office and listen to these Indian women talking about the parties they have; it's an open thing. To me, it's not normal. People are sick in a way they don't recognize. Each family is fighting for itself, and I see those problems after going through my experience.

If you want two careers in the family, you have to prepare yourselves. You accept that you're working not for yourselves but for everyone in the family. The center line draws the two lanes of the highway together; it goes on and on and on. But if you are pushed into this lifestyle the way Indian people were, there's only one way the road will go and that's to separate. Talking about teaching Indian people to work—getting a paycheck every two weeks, buying groceries, buying a car—is not talking about how working will affect family life. Everything has a by-product. The little things cause problems, then grow.

When I think about my life, the things I went through, it's almost like walking on ice at certain periods. The ice is thin, but you walk over it. You always feel insecure when you're in the middle of the pond because you know it's deep. You have a tendency to think you can make yourself lighter by holding your breath. You creep along, but in reality you're the same weight. Then you make it to the edge and leap to solid ground, and you feel good.

When you go through hard situations in life, thereafter you always come to these little ponds you have to cross. If you lived a good life before, all the way through, you don't have too many of these small ponds to cross, but you do have them. You always want to feel thankful when you get to the other side. But then again, you look at it this way: maybe it was meant to be this way. Maybe God tests each of us to find out what type of person we're making of ourselves, where we came from, or how solid we're going to be in the end.

In your lifetime, even if you grew up with a lot of people or you're non-Indian and have a lot of friends, at some time somebody will stab you in the back. Someday one of your closest friends or relations will call you down and say, "You're no good." After all the things you've been doing, something will trigger that, and thereafter they will never like you as they did before. Or they will come back but use that against you. Or they'll forgive you and return to a certain level.

Peyote and other spirits will never do that no matter what you've done wrong in this world. Peyote will still look at you at the same level you were before. If you Sun Dance, you create a center for your life. It's the same way with sweat houses and other ways of worship. You have something to go by. I Sun Dance, I go to sweat lodges, and I use peyote. That doesn't mean I walk away from the others, but if it narrowed down to one, peyote is what I would take. If I want to help someone, I take a smoke—as simple as that. I will smoke tobacco, a peace pipe, peyote, and then say, "Okay this is what it is; this is what will happen." But I must always talk about good things, not about something that will hurt someone. If you're asking for a certain thing for a certain person, you don't want to ask in a way that will hurt someone else's feelings. It's got to be equal.

When you go to religious doings, the darker parts of your life somewhat bother you. People look at your background and say, "You did that in your life; therefore, you're not a good Christian," or "You're not a good Indian." Eventually that wears out, so you get to strong ground again. You have to be extra careful not to hurt anyone or say anything out of the way, because when people are cornered they bark at you and bring out their real feelings. Those things are going to come back, and you can't really get away because you did those things.

This painful experience in my life caused me to feel a separation with my religion. It seemed it got away from me. I had to go further to reach out before I could bring it back. But I stayed with it; the problem was just in my mind. Every time I went into a meeting, I would feel this guilt. I felt people were looking at me. I listened for them to say something. If they did, that triggered this feeling: "They're talking about me. They're not accepting me. When I talk, they turn the other way and start talking. I've got to get out of here."

You really become a loner. You're by yourself. But then again, you learn that all things have to be dealt with by yourself. If I hadn't learned that, I would be depending on those people until this day. Now I can handle it by myself. It's a rough life, really. I went through it. If somebody asks me about it, I say, "Yes, let me tell you something about it." If I see a young couple breaking up and they want me to talk to them, I say, "Let me tell you the way I experienced it. This is what is going to happen." They'll sit down and listen to me because they know I went through it.

Since the time I began living with my present wife, I have learned a lot. I did many things I wouldn't normally have done. My second marriage added a lot to my life, though maybe I still would have done some things. But then again, I wish I'd never left my family. You can't experience the same happiness you had before because it's going to be based on something else. So you have to make the best of what you have now.

Maybe things have a way of finally coming together. I can go to my ex-wife now, and we discuss almost anything. She'll talk to me, too. There is no anger there; it's just a normal conversation. "How are you doing?" "How are the kids doing? Did our daughter talk to you about this?" At times I'll invite her over to the house and get our children there to talk about a problem. My wife will be there, too, with my ex-wife and our kids in the same room. We're going to talk about the problems they're having. The idea behind this is that the problem is solved right there; they can't manipulate us and we have control.

I think this way may be the only answer, where you all talk to each other. We'll sit in the same ceremony, and everybody knows that I used to be married to her. If she says, "I want you to pray for this," I'll do that, too.

I guess some people wouldn't accept that. To them, it's not normal. A lot of Indians are that way. They'll hate that person for the rest of their lives. Their spouses will hate that person. There's jealousy involved, so we don't get along. Politics get involved, too; we carry this from our homes to the outside, clear to the top level. But if we could all sit down and talk to each other and say, "Well I used to be married to that person," or, "This used to be my friend in Roosevelt," it would be a lot better.

I have to maintain a neutral position no matter what. If the people on the other side of the fence don't talk back to me, I still have to talk to them. Some people I say hello to don't say anything back. I keep saying that: "How are you?" It's just the way it is. People are going to judge you by what you are.

I was brought up this way. You don't listen to what a person says when they talk about someone else; you listen to him about him. When you express a negative feeling about another person, you are talking about yourself. When I say, "He's no good, he's a son of a bitch," and all that, I am talking about me. So when you talk about people, you must always talk about good things. Otherwise they are going to think you are that way, too. So when you listen to people talk, you know they are that way, too.

In a ceremony, things go from left to right. Whatever goes by you one way is going to come back the other way. So whatever you say when you pray and talk, make sure you say something good because it's going to come back to you. I think the bottom line is how we survive in this world is so simple—it's meant for everybody, but not everybody expects it.

Someday you're going to find that whatever you're looking for isn't that hard to find. It's so simple. You think that it's something really beyond you, but someday you'll see that answer and feel so stupid. It's simple; how come I didn't think of that? God works that way, too. The complications we go through were not made by him.

Museum Director

In about 1980, I became museum director of the Ute Tribal Museum. I took over for Fred Coneta. I was qualified because of my knowledge about Indian life, being part of Indian religious groups, and having discipline in those ways. At the museum, we moved from one building to the other, but we basically kept the museum the same as before. We don't collect any items that are old; we try to stay away from that.

In 1983, I worked on the tail-end of the Fremont excavation near Richfield. We had the state archeologist, namely Jim Duykman, giving archeology classes in Vernal to a group of us. To become certified, we were required to participate in an excavation. So we divided into two sections; the first would come down to Richfield for one week; the following week the others would come down. They had some Paiutes there from the Richfield area that were trained to do excavations. I didn't want to stay for a long period of time, so I just stayed one week in June or July. The weather was really hot, too, really hot. It would cool down a little bit if we had a breeze.

We'd do the regular archeological things, a lot of measuring, labeling, a lot of screening, making sure to report every little thing, drawing diagrams, taking pictures. Excavation is a slow process, and that's what we did. In the area I was in, there was a metate—a stone used for grinding grains—found. We scraped back the dirt from around it, kept working down to the next level, like an altitude measurement in centimeters. You'd get to the wall, go down, note different colorations of the dirt, hit a hard floor, go beyond that, here's another hard floor. I enjoyed it. We stayed at the Wagon Wheel Motel in Richfield. They turned the shower room into a lab.

There's a fellow, who has a degree, who carves arrowheads, and he explains how the rock will split a certain way; it's all scientific the way he explains that. Now, in the old days, there was an Indian from whom the professor is learning how to carve arrowheads. The Indian couldn't have explained the rock breaking in a scientific way, and yet the professor is learning from him. So who has what?

In between the academic way and the Indian way, there is a blank area that represents the spiritual part. You could put almost anything in there. The professor describes it the way he describes it. Then I, being on this side, accept what he is explaining; but then again I widen it out because I insert this blank space into that, the way that I learned it. For instance, if we are talking about human remains or human bones, I accept the fact that they belong to a person who was alive like any person today. But when the person died, the spirit left that. Archeologists accept that, or they give that definition to that piece of bone sitting there.

But I would say, "No, they did not leave that piece of bone completely." Because to me that bone has its own spirit, which did not make that bone part of another, but still has the power that made the bone move when it was alive. If I do something with that bone, it somewhat is tied to the spirit that left. So if I do something wrong with the bone, it will pull the spirit back. The spirit will come to me in a different form, through dreams or through something that blocks whatever I'm doing, or to make me pay for things that I do wrong. So if I bother human remains—if it's in the grave, it's not to be bothered—if I start doing that, I eventually will come face to face with whoever the bone belonged to. So that area is there.

But the archeologist won't see that—certain archeologists will, I'm not saying they're all like that. Archeologists seem to be coming around to that but not because of what they believe but because of what the law says. The laws determine how they should handle this.

Some people are saying, "We have respect for you, so we will return these bones to you rather than display them." So the law says something about it. But on the other hand, do they actually believe that? I'm watching both sides of it. Indian people watch because the archeologists might not actually believe it. Then, if the law changes, the archeologists will say, "Forget that." They have a tendency to change that quickly.

They respect the law first; then me; then the bones. The way we look at it, we respect the bones, then ourselves, then the law last. That's the way we believe.

I enjoyed museum work. I think it brought me full circle. As a museum director, I worked in the field assisting archeologists, which brought me back home again. The work was a language I understood, a language that talked to me in some ways and knew how I felt.

Still, museum work had its frustrations because of the way people misunderstood Indians. I had a heated discussion with a social worker who had just been hired. He had this magnificent idea to create jobs for the Indian people. So he wrote a proposal—a culturally based program to motivate the Indian people so they can think a certain way, but they're going to have work. It sounded so easy. In fact, it had been tried several times.

I told him, "This has been tried before and it didn't work, and I'll tell you why. If I had this same proposal you've submitted and took it before the council, they'd tell me no. But because you're a white person and you took it in there, they would say okay."

He said, "No, it doesn't work that way."

I said, "Yes it does, because I used to do that trick, too. I know that trick. When I was a tribal planner, I used to do that trick. I'd put together a proposal, then give it to a non-Indian and say, 'Take it in there. Present it to them.' If I took it in, they'd say no. But it's so easy for the non-Indian."

I don't know why; this, I don't have an answer for—why Indian people are that way in high positions. Do they accept those proposals because they don't want to be labeled as ignorant by this white person who brings it in? Or maybe they don't know what level they're at; they play the role of being the boss, the big shot, the council member. But do they really know what they are doing? I think that tendency goes back to how tribal leaders are selected.

His proposal wouldn't work, the way I looked at it, because people are people. You cannot sit down and write out a plan and figure that everybody will respond to whatever you present like a machine. If I wrote out a job description and expected you to do all of that in a given time, and expected you to produce in this way, I would be wrong because there's a missing part to everything. People have feelings; you've got to deal with people on an individual basis. You've got to talk to the people, know the people, and once you get to know all of that you're going to know what will fit. The commitment's going to come from the people themselves. This sounded like it would be easy. Everybody was going to be there with a shovel at eight o'clock in the morning sharp, all gung ho.

What he wanted was a new museum, a cultural center. The council accepted that but then he wanted to know if I concurred. When I talked to him, I said, "I didn't even look at the proposal. I don't even know what's there. How could I agree when I don't know what's in it? I'm against the whole idea."

Most of the time I will go along with things. If I can read a proposal first, I will find out if it's going to be strong or weak. But if I don't look at it, if I don't see it up front, I have to reject it because I don't know. I can't say, "Well, let's try it." The plan was ridiculous.

I asked him, "Who's going to pay them? There's nothing there to say they'll get money from here or there. Are you expecting people to come in? From where? Who's going to bring them in? Do you charge admission? Where are the people going to come from? From Salt Lake City or where? Are they going to be the people who come along the road and stop? How many people come in during the summer? Winter? How many white people in the Uintah Basin will come to an Indian doings—and pay? They're going to say, 'Shit, I'm not going to pay no Indian.' That's what they're going to say."

This proposal never took into consideration how we live on the reservation and in the Uintah Basin, or the way we think about things. Our thinking blocks the whole thing. These white people could set up a museum; they do set up Indian museums. But I've lived among Uintah Basin people all my life. I know how they think.

The Human Side of Things

For some time, my wife and our daughter and I lived in the house that had been my father's on his allotment near Neola. After a few years of fixing it up, my sisters and brothers said, "Well, since we all have homes, you can have that house." So that was fine up until the mid-1980s.

Then one of them said to me, "You have to buy that house if you're going to live there." They had told me some years before that I could have it; but now two sisters got together and said, "You've got to pay us for that." So the others went along.

I got someone to assess the value of the house. The going rate in Neola was about $30,000. I had put a lot of money into fixing up the house because it was almost ruined when I moved in. When the assessor came, he said I had to pay again for that in value.

All this happened just about the time the large dividends ended, when people were no longer getting money from natural resource royalties. I had to turn around and borrow from a bank, and give each one of my sisters and my brother what they wanted. I'm still paying the bank to this day. It's a tough world. I wish they had done that in 1976 when the dividend money was coming in. Why wait until it almost ends and then decide that? So that's one of my reasons why I've got to keep working. I've got to work, and I've got to do this and that—it's a tough world. When you get by yourself, you have to do it by yourself; but I appreciate everything, too. I still love my sisters and my brother, even though the problem with the house happened, because it gave me the total ownership of the house in later years. So all is well.

My brother was elected chairman of the Business Committee in 1989. I have a sister working in the education department, another who is a purchasing clerk, and another working for the tribe in another capacity, too—but we didn't get into such positions overnight. My brother had never worked for the tribe in his life. He worked for Mountain Bell for twelve years, then got elected as tribal chairman.

At the moment, I don't want to have anything to do with politics. When the reform movement started and they were going to do away with the council, they asked me to chair the meeting that began the whole process. When they were through, and everything went according to plan, they didn't want to listen to me any more. The plan I had, which went along with the reforms, was discarded. They said, "We're going to do it our way."

My idea was that you start off by changing the constitutional bylaws, updating them to the point where everything runs the way business should be run today. We need better control of our governing body. We need to change our voting system so we can elect the best of the membership. The way it is now, any person who resides on the reservation for at least one year and is at least twenty-one years of age can get in. That's what I told them. I still believe that way. "Do away with the band system. Let's elect the council by district," I said. "If we do it by district, certain families don't have control anymore. Everybody is part of it." Nothing in government has changed since the election. That's why I don't want to be a part of it.

In my spiritual or Indian life, I don't think my changes in residence or position during the 1970s or 1980s made any difference. You do a lot of other things, like changing positions, getting away from the reservation, living in the city, all of that. But the way that you remain with your religion never changes; it's a stationary thing. You are only a small part of it. Religion is bigger than you. If you feel that the religion is inside of you, then you would have a tendency to feel the other way, that you are bigger than it.

I think that's a difference with a lot of Indian people. When they use religion, they tell it what to do; they become bigger than it. Then they say, "Well, I live by that because I asked this to happen, and it happened." Really, when you look at it, it's not that way. Religion is bigger than me. I cannot tell it what to do. But I can do things, and say, "Will you help me?" My lifestyle made no change in that, no change whatsoever.

You have to recognize the simple fact that all prayers are answered either yes or no. People say, "God never answers my prayers." Sure, he did. He said no. Being that he's superior to everything in this world, and being that he's your father, he knows what would hurt you or make you happy.

It's like a young boy asking for a knife from his father, saying, "Dad, let me have a knife." The father knows he's going to cut himself or hurt somebody, so he says no. Or if you ask your mother or father, "Let me drive the car to school today," your parent knows you're going to wreck it and says no.

So you have to take God that way, too. Whatever you ask from a superior being, you have to accept the fact that sometimes he will say no. No means no. You can't walk away from God either.

That reminds me of a story, a joke. A praying man was walking along a hill, and all of a sudden he fell off. As he fell, he grabbed hold of a branch that was sticking out. Hanging there, he said, "God, please help me."

And God talked to him. "What do you want?"

Meanwhile, he was hanging on to that thing and it was coming loose. He was going to fall. He said, "God, can you help me? What should I do?"

God answered, "Turn loose. Let go."

The man answered back really quick and said, "Is there anybody else up there who can help me?"

People sometimes look at prayer that way, and that's not the way to be. The first person to answer is the one you're talking to; there's nobody else there. If you say there is, you don't believe in him.

But as you get older, I think the spiritual way becomes stronger. You begin to feel a human side of things. Your relationship with people has a tenderness to it, whereas in your younger years you weren't paying too much attention, though if people expressed it you might see it. For instance, people talk about suffering, pain. You never realize it until you've suffered. Then when you've finally experienced what suffering is, you know; you've matured.

You mature into areas that make you aware of what being old and being sensitive mean: love for things, love for people. There are no boundaries to it. You love people just for what they are, not for what color their skin is, but for what's inside of them. You begin to see things like that. It is hard to face a world where there's a difference just because of race.

True, you advance from one level to another. I think by going out and meeting people, or working in different areas, it gives you a different outlook on your religion and life. If I don't look at my beliefs from another point of view, I'm set in my ways. Eventually that's damaging. You begin to find that it's a matter of interpretation. When I talk to people, I can explain religion in a different way so they can really understand.

I will never find an instructor who will teach me the exact thing I'm looking for. If it's from a human, it's not what I need. I learn from ceremony. I have to sacrifice, too. I have to give my time, my life, to it. It would never enter my mind to quit. I enjoy doing it.

In your later years you begin to notice that a lot of people are having a hard time. You wonder, "How come they don't do it right?" They say that the hardest thing in the world to do is to watch somebody do something, and they are doing it wrong. You want to say something. The hardest thing is to keep your mouth shut. It's somewhat like that when you become separated from the rest of them, you say,

"How come? I wish they could do it this other way." In later years, from such experience, you develop patience.

But my people use religion this way, too. If it's any religious doings such as the Sun Dance, there might be only two hundred people involved. The rest don't believe in it. But books say, "Ute Indians have their Sun Dance." It's only a small group. Peyote ceremonies are the same way; the sweat lodge the same way. So maybe eighty percent of them are just Indians by blood because they're born into it. The religious groups are fairly separate, but there are a few of us that go all the way around. I go to Sun Dance, I go to sweats, I go to peyote ceremonies, and I go to powwows. Then, at times, I go to Christian churches.

I can pray just as well in a Sun Dance as I can in a sweat lodge or in a peyote teepee. Those people who stay with one, will say, "This is the only way; this is the right way." But that's not true because they don't know. They are in a vacuum.

Being the way I am, the outcome is really this: how you live is what really makes the difference; that's what determines how good your way really is.

I think if you work at all the religious ceremonies equally, you distribute yourself, it's all the same. The basic premise of all religion is the same—how you feel and how you express yourself. How close to God do you get? The rest follows easily. It is almost like you have to start with the center part first in order to develop the rest. You cannot develop the outside, then come into the center. It has to go from the center out. For me, it worked that way.

I think as time goes on, too, you begin to balance out your friends and put them at an equal level with everything that you have. You have friends on the reservation and friends over here in the city. You want to learn about something, so you utilize people. Friends are there to help you whether they know it or not. But you don't want to hurt them or use them in a way that hurts your relationship. None of my friends is lower than the other; they're all the same. Whatever they do in life, whatever they're good at, that is their gift.

ARTIFACTS, HEIRLOOMS, AND ACQUAINTANCES

War bonnet that belonged to Chief John Duncan, Ute name Ungatavinekent. He was one the last chiefs of the Ute Tribe.
He was the great-grandfather of Clifford Duncan. Photographed at Clifford Duncan's home in Neola, Utah.

NOVEMBER 25, 2016

Dance stick that a Men's Traditional Dancer would dance with. Photographed at Clifford Duncan's home in Neola, Utah.

NOVEMBER 25, 2016

Clifford Duncan made this dance bustle for his grandson. It is an old-style traditional bustle.
Photographed at Clifford Duncan's home in Neola, Utah.

NOVEMBER 25, 2016

Clifford Duncan made this cedar bag. He would dance with it and also use it to put his cedar in for ceremonial use. Photographed at Clifford Duncan's home in Neola, Utah.

NOVEMBER 25, 2016

A dance staff is used to bring in dancers during a powwow. Photographed at Clifford Duncan's home in Neola, Utah.

NOVEMBER 25, 2016

Clifford Duncan's eagle staff, which is used to bring in the dancers during Grand Entry.

Photographed at Clifford Duncan's home in Neola, Utah.

NOVEMBER 25, 2016

Old photograph of Clifford Duncan and the Utah Episcopal Bishop Carolyn Tanner Irish. Photographed at Clifford Duncan's home in Neola, Utah.

NOVEMBER 25, 2016

Painting by Clifford Duncan next to ceremonial staffs. Photographed at Clifford Duncan's home in Neola, Utah.

NOVEMBER 25, 2016

Clifford Duncan with the Dalai Lama in Salt Lake City circa 1990. Photographed at Clifford Duncan's home in Neola, Utah.

NOVEMBER 25, 2016

The little boy in the vest is Clifford Duncan's father, Ivan Duncan.
Photographed at Clifford Duncan's home, Neola, Utah.

NOVEMBER 25, 2016

Clifford's father, Ivan Duncan, is the fourth from the right. Photographed at Clifford Duncan's home in Neola, Utah.

NOVEMBER 25, 2016

Clifford Duncan is the second from the left. This image was taken in Oklahoma with Kiowa and Apache men.
Photographed at Clifford Duncan's home in Neola, Utah.

NOVEMBER 25, 2016

Clifford Duncan's "adopted" mother and father through ceremony, Nora Parker and Baldwin Parker Sr., in Whiterocks, Utah, circa 1960. They came up from Cache, Oklahoma, and spent time with Clifford at his home in Neola, Utah. Photographed at Clifford Duncan's home in Neola, Utah.

NOVEMBER 25, 2016

Painting

When you do a painting, it feels like you belong to it and it belongs to you. It's a relationship. Sometimes I do symbolic paintings tied into religion or my way of life. Those type of paintings I really hate to part with, but I did part with some recently. A lady bought a number of them for several hundred dollars and took them to California. I don't know what happened to them.

I'm in my own world when I paint because I'm doing it the way I feel. The colors that I use are the colors that I feel. If I put them in the right order, the right area, the right time, the right place, they become a picture. You notice some paintings have too much red, too much blue—it throws it off. You learn to place the right amount of color on a picture. To get a response, you have to do that.

I centralize my thinking on that; what object in a painting is going to pull you? It's not the whole painting that's going to pull you, but one detail that's really good. Color is going to be that way, too. People paint pictures of war using colors to reflect that.

I used to do a lot of Indian paintings. Lately I've worked with contemporary subjects like landscapes, scenery, or painting an object—like a moccasin by itself, a still-life, or maybe a warbonnet sitting alone. It's still Indian but it's today; it's a style used today. I mix realistic painting and the symbolic painting, stylized painting. I try to put them together.

For me, art is expressive, but on the other hand I might paint about a subject that is happening out there. At certain times I might paint a Sun Dance scene, how people see that. It might not really be my experience. A Southern Cheyenne might see that painting and, right now, connect; it's for them I do that, not for me. At times I paint that way.

I'm not going to put everything about me in a painting. I have to leave something for myself. I like painting; painting completes a sketch. A sketch is only an outline even if it's a really good sketch. A lot of people can sketch and do a good job because you're not dealing with colors, merely black and white. You can shade with black and that's it; there's nothing to it. Everybody can do that. Painting covers the sketch. Sketching is merely the first stage, outlining what's going to be there. But finding the colors for that painting to paint itself is what makes the picture complete. I am putting on that board my way of looking at it, the subject, my feeling about it.

I like winter, I like snow. I like how it makes me feel as I watch snow drift, pile up. It changes; it has a rhythm to it, a motion that really digs down into you. If it gets really cold, you build up a resistance against that and it changes. You find that cold is not cold; cold has sort of a solid effect on a person—you can break it, it snaps. The hurting part is the first of cold weather when the temperature drops; it hurts down to the bone. After you go through that stage, it's just cold. The words freeze as they come out of your mouth; you can actually read them. I like to paint snow; it takes a certain feeling. Of all the seasons in painting scenery, snow is the best.

I also make flutes, and I made a bustle for an exhibit. I'm working on flint-napping now, too. I made a spear. I'm going to make a certain type about four feet long with a hook on the end; it's what the Anasazi used to use to hunt. They have those in the museums. On the end of the spear there's an indented circle, and that's where it hooks in. When you throw it, the curve gives it extra push. They used to hunt mammoth elephants and big bison.

I'm going to hunt dinosaurs with my weapon in Vernal. I have a hunting license for either sex, so I can pick out the closest target. That's what the park is for, Dinosaur Park. (Just kidding.)

22

Healing Ceremonies

On the Goshute Reservation a few years ago, a man was sick. A spiritual doctor had been called. Then, toward the end of the ceremony, he couldn't help him anymore. The shaman said, "Brother Clifford, I want you to help me." Upon agreeing to try, I proceeded to carry the ceremony from where he left it off.

I had to depend totally on my belief, and I did it. I shouldn't say I did it; something or someone acted through me. But I believe in myself and in what I'm doing. Why would a person who believes ever be lost? You just go back to where you started and start from there.

Nothing is solved by argument. You have to start at the beginning. I find peyote is like a man who will listen to me, my counselor, my director. I take it into myself; then I can figure out where the weakness is. I have my teacher, my instructor. I creep the information through my mind. Peyote will show you what you already know. It will never turn its back on you like a human will.

If I am asked to perform a ceremony, especially if I am asked within a ceremony, that is a total commitment. I cannot back out; I cannot change the dates. Once it's set, it's set; rain or shine, I would have to follow through. That's usually how that works. With ordinary promises, it would be different. But the way we understand the system, you will be judged on how you live up to your words within a ceremony. That's how languages are used, too, to keep you from going astray.

People ask me to conduct a service if they are acquainted with me or if they know I conduct services. Also they consider the type of ceremonies you perform. Some healers will be known for working with people who are sick with pneumonia. Some are good working with people who have a difficult time with family life, or they're not living right. Then you can get into the serious type of illnesses. Once others find out that person does that, they will call on them to do that for them, too.

There are different levels of healing, too. All road men cannot be the same; all people who conduct services are not the same. The years of experience matter for each one, and the family line, too; certain families are known for certain things.

I think I'm somewhat a general practitioner. I've been to the Cree Reservation to conduct ceremonies several times. One was a memorial meeting. The mother had died, and they wanted to have a special memorial service for the family several months after her death. They asked me to go there and pray for the children, grandchildren, the immediate family of that lady. I did that.

At times we have a thanksgiving meeting, giving thanks to the Creator for the struggles they went through. If they had a meeting earlier and everything turned out well for them, then we meet again to say thank you. They have birthday meetings, too.

What goes on within the meeting is a simple thing, really, but it's a matter of how you go about it. If you and I sat down together somewhere, and we combined our efforts in the way that we think, the way we bring ourselves together, something good would come out of that. When families get together and all think about one thing, it will come out that way, but it will take someone within that group to lead. You could lead by praying or by talking to people.

When you pray, you're praying to the Man Up Above or the Great Spirit. People have respect for that person or spirit you're talking to. In fact, they will not even think of doubting you; that's how you draw them in. So you ask him for a cure for this person; please help us. At the same time, you ask that they'll live the rest of their lives in good health.

This story comes to my mind. I was in Idaho one time and a Sioux, an elderly man who was a chief, talked to me. He told me how people used to do healings a long time ago.

"Your mind is strong. Your prayers are strong," he said. "Years ago we used to have our meetings in a different way. We had better control of people; nowadays our control is kind of weak. Years ago, a man could fill up a teepee with followers and they would all sit. Whatever the chief told them, they would do it exactly as told. If he told everybody to keep quiet, they would keep quiet. That's how they believed in this man.

"So there would come a time in the ceremony when he would ask of them certain things. He would ask the people, 'I want you to think with me that it's going to be this way.' He'd say, 'There's a sick man here, and he is either going to make it or he's going to die.' The chief tells the people it's that way—a man is going to live or die.

"Then he would say, 'We're at the point where we're going to bring him back to health, but it's going to take each one of you.' He would take a plume and tell the people, 'When this eagle plume lands on the ground, it's going to land on the bottom, then it's going to fall. If it falls, this man is going to die. If it stands there for a few seconds or minutes, he's going to make it. Here is what I want you to do. Think real hard that this feather is not going to fall.'"

That's what he would tell them, how to think together. Then he would throw it. The eagle plume goes up in the air, hits the ground—and the amazing thing was, he told me, that the feather never fell. It stood in one place, straight up. Eventually the chief would say, "Okay," and then it would fall. This Sioux told me that's how strong your mind can be. That is spiritual energy at work.

In a way, Indian religion is based on how people can work together. Peyote helps that cause. It is the only thing we have left today that can control people in the way that they conduct services in a systemized manner. That's why it is a spirit that accomplishes a lot. It's a spirit that's like a person, and you should treat peyote like a person. He comes to your house as an orphan. You accept him as a brother. You take care of him and show him around. You treat him well, and he's going to treat you well. He's going to give you a lot of things, and bring friends to you, too. He comes to listen to you talk; he comes to listen to you sing. You are singing to him; he knows you can sing. That's the way it is, the relationship with peyote.

Dealing with spiritual things is not far away; it's within reach, you can touch it—and yet seems so far away. I always tell my people this: you're going to walk around the world looking for a quick healing if you're sick. You're going to try to find something that will heal you overnight. Or you're going to look for something good, and follow here and there looking for it. One day you're going to come back from the west, the east, and take a good look at yourself and find out then that, all the time, what you were looking for is inside of you; that's where it is. The thing that's going to make you well, the thing that's going to make you happy, is inside of you. No one else had it for you. You had it all the time.

If you go to a medicine man or go to another way of life, you're going to find that when you come back, it's going to be so simple. I've experienced that myself. That's why I believe that God is going to be the one to help. He put something inside each person to help them or others. Each one of us will have that gift.

For instance, if I do a painting I'm going to put a little bit of me in it. When you look at it, you're going to say, "He did it," because it makes you feel a certain way. God does the same thing with you or me. Inside of us is a little bit of him.

The basics of ceremony are simply that—all manmade things have a tendency to die. If you believe in a certain man, when he dies, you die too. If he's the one that told you a certain thing and you believe in that and him, you have no other place to turn because he's gone. But if you believe in something that's everlasting, if you believe in God, if you believe in the sun, then when you die, it all continues. There's no end to it. So you have a choice: believe in a man or believe in God, the Holy Spirit, the Great Spirit, so many names.

One time I was talking to a group of elders and asked, "Why can't I give God a name? Why can't I call him George? People call me by my name. Why can't we just say, Bobby or Joey? 'Hey Joey, come here.'"

God can laugh, too. Why do people go to God and cry and tell him all the worries they have? How come every time they pray they're asking for something? Why not go to God and sit down and say, "Let's laugh together. This is what I did." Maybe he likes to laugh, too.

Why can't you treat God the way you treat people? He made me so I would end up like this. He has a sense of humor, too, because he made me. He had a little fun in making me, too—look at me.

When God made this world, he created people in all dimensions. This is one dimension. You and I are here; we see each other. There's another world, another group of people, which we don't see. These little ones are there. I call them little people. They live in the earth and they come up. The way I picture them, they're dressed the way old-time Indians used to dress. They depend totally on nature.

There is this physical world, the spirit world, and an in-between world. The in-between world is where the little people live. They can become a spirit or they can become like us. Then you can see them and hear them. When you walk through an area, you can feel someone watching you; they are the ones watching. During the night you hear songs; they are the ones singing. Or in a dream you can see them coming; or you can actually feel them standing there. Children have a tendency to be closer to them than adults. You hear people talking about their kids laughing and playing with someone, someone is in the baby's room—those are little people.

The Rocky Boy, Montana, ceremony I conducted recently was no different than the meetings here—a peyote ceremony. A Cree boy who has been here for several years married one of my nieces, and he goes to meetings, and my niece also goes to meetings. They have children. His father lives in Rocky Boy. So we had a ceremony for the birthday of the oldest child.

Since I am the uncle, he said, "We want you to be there if you can make it." The way I felt about it, that niece of mine lost her mother several years ago and her father was in Arizona. My sister was sick and died. Her husband left her and remarried, and that was it.

The way that Indian people look at it, I'm the oldest one in the family now. My father died, my sisters, one brother, so I automatically moved up to the position of the one responsible for those sisters; that's my responsibility. If my sister dies, I'm responsible for my nieces, my nephews.

When I go to ceremonies, I have to pray for each of them because they don't have a mother or father there for them. When they have children, they are my grandchildren. Even though they're my nieces, I'm their dad and their kids are my grandchildren. When I go somewhere, such as a ceremony they sponsor, I have to go with the idea that I am there to support them, also to tell my niece how other groups do things. If there's going to be any cultural difference in the way they do things, I explain, "Our family's this way. This is the way this ties in with that."

Then if they give the baby an Indian name in the ceremony, I have to know that name because I will have to refer to it later on. This is a spiritual name—I have an Indian name, too—if I pray for that person, if they're sick, I have to use that Indian name. That's why we have Indian names. That's why I have to go to these ceremonies. It's a spiritual law or regulation that you cannot get too far away from; you have to respond to it. Whenever one of these occasions comes up, I have to say, "Well, I'm going to do that. That's number one." That's a spiritual commitment.

The door to life leads into the other world. My people say there are two people standing there. They are the ones you're going to talk to before you go through the door. They are Indian, and dressed completely in red. Their buckskin outfits are red; their faces are red, and also their hair. They are the eternal beings, a man and a woman. That's what my people say.

When they see a child, something pure, come to the door, they let it go through and ask no questions. A person who has touched a lot of things in life—a germ, a way of life, mistakes you've made, your experiences—that person is *nurischanikah*. But the young one is free of all things, and it is easier for a child to pass through that door.

There's a song we use in ceremonies that talks about life beyond the end of the elderly age, beyond our life here. They say you have a choice; if you go to one side, you go into the Happy Hunting Ground. If you go to the other side, you're going to live beyond that fourth section of a normal life. So that's what we pray for; you've got to be strong enough to go beyond your time, to be able to choose to go beyond that.

Last week I thought I was getting old: "I'm an elder. I can go on a trip with the senior citizens." I said that last week. I went to Rocky Boy. I met this old man, introduced by one of his grandchildren. His last name was Chiefstick. This old man talked to me.

"Where are you from?"

"Utah."

"Good."

Regular conversation, really good; he talked English, too. It was afterward when they told me how old he was that I felt really young—he's one hundred and four years old. Compared to that, I've got a long way to go yet. I'm just a young kid.

23

Government and Peyote

On April 17, 1990, the United States Supreme Court ruled on a case called *Employment Division, Department of Human Resources of Oregon et al vs. Smith et al.* The decision of the Supreme Court was that state legislatures may prohibit members of the Native American Church from using peyote, or they may enact express legislative exemption for the sacramental use of peyote.

Actually, that's how we read it; but what happened in this case was that in Oregon a man named Smith, Al Smith, and another man named Black, worked for this drug counseling program in Oregon. They got fired, evidently, because they told their employer that they used peyote in Native American Church services. One was an Indian. The other wasn't; but they both carried Native American Church membership cards.

Later Smith and Black went to the unemployment office and filed for unemployment, but the division there refused them, so they took the matter to court. They were saying that peyote was not really a drug as far as Indians were concerned. Since they had used it only in Native American Church ceremonies, that use should be exempted.

It so happened that Oregon had no exemptions, but the federal Drug Enforcement Administration has exemptions; it's a federal law. It's up to each state to have its own laws. If the state says you can't use peyote, then that becomes the law within that state, but only on state land. Oregon didn't have a law. So Smith and Black carried this issue, and the first time, I think, they won the case. Then Oregon came back again, and the judge reversed the decision. Then the men wanted to take it to the Supreme Court, and that's how it ended up there. When it hit the Supreme Court, the decision said all states will have to make rulings on these exemptions.

The Native American Church got involved because of the peyote. Actually, it was those two men involved in the controversy, but they used the Native American Church as a crutch. There is nothing wrong with the peyote ceremony; this has nothing to do with it. The Native American Church went in as a friend of the court; they did not get involved in the case itself. However, it affected all members of the Native American Church throughout the country, as they became aware of the possibility that states would prohibit the use of peyote.

Right after that, the Native American Church had a big meeting, the North American group. I went to that meeting, and they talked about that case. One suggestion was that Indians could go back to their respective states and work with the legislatures to see if they could have an exemption for each state not already exempted. That way, they could take care of any future problems at the state level.

In Utah, we just kind of let it go. Then in June or July Christopher Smart, a reporter at the *Salt Lake Tribune*, got in touch with the Division of Indian Affairs in Salt Lake City and asked to talk with someone about this case in Washington. So they referred him to me. He called me, and I talked to him. In the newspaper it came out that he had met with the attorney general, and the attorney general was putting together a policy in reference to peyote as exempted in the Native American Church.

Smart asked what we were going to do, or how people would be affected on reservations. I told him that it does not really affect us; state law cannot be applied on Indian reservations because reservations have federal status. However, Indian people in the Salt Lake City area would be hurt because they have an organization called the Native American Church of the Wasatch Front, mainly consisting of Navajos. Those are the ones who would be affected by a new law because they would have to comply.

Later on we had a meeting with the attorney general, Paul Van Dam, and one of his staff attorneys, Paula Smith. Also John Powless, then-director of Indian Affairs, and his assistant attended. At that meeting I explained to the attorney general what the Native American Church is, what ceremonies are involved, what the whole thing means within the ceremony, how we use peyote, and what part it plays. I explained to him all of that, and he was very much pleased with that kind of information because I guess he'd heard from one side—but not from the Indian side, that's what he said.

Later I met with Beverly Evans, a senator representing Uintah-Duchesne and Summit Counties. She wanted to put together arguments to present during the legislative session. She was going to sponsor that bill. I talked to her later on. In the meantime, I had a meeting with Enid Greene, chief of staff for the governor. John Powless and his assistant were present, and Beverly Evans was there, too. We went over the things the bill would contain and that was it. So we started putting it together.

Then last week they gave me a copy of a rough draft of the bill itself. One part I didn't like regarded the amount of peyote that would be sent out of state if we manufactured it. But there's no manufacturing of peyote here; it grows in Texas. So I called in and told them, "Delete lines nine to thirteen on page two." I guess the same afternoon they got a docket number for the bill. Tomorrow we have another meeting.

In the meantime we did this: we wrote letters to all the tribes within the state, those that use the peyote, inviting them to Salt Lake to have an informational meeting. We intended to explain to them what we had been doing and ask support from them. That includes the Navajos, the Southern Utes, the Shoshones, the Goshutes, the Paiutes, and the Utes.

Then I learned that Steve Moore, the attorney for the northern area's Native American Rights Fund, had changed his advice. (He's an Indian attorney who works on behalf of Indian tribes throughout the country, visiting from Boulder, Colorado.) Steve said that it may not be the time to introduce this legislation because the drug war is at its strongest point. Therefore, the legislature may downgrade anything that's a drug; they might make a big criminal case out of it, too. Anyway that's what he said. Tomorrow at the meeting the question's going to be whether we carry through or not. If they vote no on it, we're going to pull the bill.

What had happened before the Supreme Court decision is this: state ordinances had not made an exemption, but they followed the federal exemption law. The federal exemption law said that Native American Church people would be exempted. So why raise the issue? That's going to be the question tomorrow. But I don't think the Indian people know about that because I'm the only one who's really been keeping up.

Peyote grows in the southern part of Texas. The state of Texas has an exemption law that says Indians can use peyote as long as they're not less than twenty-five percent Indian blood. The law deals with dealers; the dealers have to be licensed. They cut and dry peyote, and they keep a record of how many peyote they cut. These are special dealers that ship only to Native American Church members.

Then each tribe has what they call custodians. In my tribe there are three custodians—I'm one and there are two others. We're the only ones authorized according to the Austin office in Texas to make purchases by mail. So we write to them and say, "Okay, we want so many peyote." When they send the peyote, the man who supplies it sends a copy of the receipt or authorization slip, a copy to Austin, Texas, and a copy to us, and they keep a copy. So they know how much peyote comes from Texas to us. Peyote's not harvested here, so that's why I said to delete that section. Its manufacture has nothing to do with us.

Steve Moore provided all the different states' exemption laws so we could see how they were written. In the meantime, Emerson Jackson, who is with the Native American Church for North America, had been conversing with Steve Moore. Somehow Steve's opinion changed along the way.

I don't understand why Steve Moore didn't say this wasn't necessary at the beginning. Why did he do it at the last minute? There's something going on there that I don't know anything about; I think it's kind of like politics. What I'm going to tell them tomorrow is this: that we can drop it. I have all the information. I've been carrying this all the way through, and the Division of Indian Affairs has been carrying it. Together we've been doing it. We'll drop it, but we'll keep it close to us. If it ever rises again, we'll pick it up again from that point. I will pick it up again; I'm going to carry it through. That's what I've been thinking, and that's what I'm going to tell them tomorrow.

In the meantime I'll draft up my own bill and say, "Okay, here's the way it's going to be written," and give it to Beverly Evans or whoever will sponsor it.

24

Powwow

I like the idea that white people are taking an interest in Indian ways, mainly because I think it's one way to preserve our culture. But there are so many concentric circles, and the white people are not in the center—they are in the outer circles. The center must remain Indian. There are a lot of Indian people who are not in the center either; but as long as they can stay close to the circle—fine.

The Indian way is becoming more generic. Navajos never did powwow dances, but now that is taking place. We should study this Indian trend because we're making a mistake. If something is really authentic to a group, why not say, "This is from the Muscalooso tribe," or, "This is Apache, Kiowa, Navajo, or Ute." The circle has enlarged, looped out, out, out. Somewhere it has to pick up a white person, too. That's where the change is going to take place.

Why can't we use a term—say the Native American Church—but have a different type of organization, which is composed in a broader sense than it is now? I can't see it the way most Indian people see it, and yet I can.

If I tell them, "That's wrong," they say, "No, that's the way it is." I think I know where their attitude is coming from. They want to be the ones who say, "I take care of it; that belongs to me." That's why they say no white people can come into peyote ceremonies. They're not looking at all the details going on in people's lives through intermarriage and the next generation. You've got to cut that thing right clear in the middle, and say, "You don't own that."

Everyone, however, can attend a powwow. Powwow serves several purposes. Indian identity is one purpose. Also, the main thing I see with Indian people that travel the circuit from powwow to powwow every year throughout different parts of the country, is that powwow serves as a place to socialize, a place for fellowship and visiting. We create a group of people that are identified through powwow as their structure. They're powwow people.

For instance, one of my great uncles died, then we had a giveaway last year; he was not really part of powwow, but his wife, Katie, was. His name was Dick McKuen. Katie McKuen was a powwow lady. They would travel all over the country; she would dance with the elders, and sometimes she would win a prize. The older people from other areas knew her; at times maybe she would be involved in hand games. They knew her there, too. So powwow means that, too.

Sometimes, too, people use these gatherings as a means of reaching out spiritually; it's a spiritual renewal. If a person doesn't feel well, or is lonely, or is going through a depression, or they lose their loved ones, or they're sick, they go to these powwows. The idea behind it is you forget about your sickness; you forget about your problems. With the spirit that is coming from the powwow circle, you get well; you are blessed by the songs, the scene of people there, the spirits of the people there. Everybody's united; they're all there for one reason—to support the Indian powwow. Powwow has a great spirit, a spirit by itself; so that's why people sometimes use it in that manner.

There's also a time when they have giveaways. A giveaway is somewhat like a giving of oneself, but in material goods. They give to people that they know, or maybe it's a family thing where people get together to recognize each other, or to give Indian names, or even to initiate new members into the powwow circle, the Indian circle.

In powwows you find that proper dress seems to be the main thing, too, because you are wearing feathers, or you are wearing beaded clothes, or you are wearing bustles, which you don't ordinarily wear in everyday life. Everything you wear has a certain significance, tying in with traditional-type dancing, or it may be a fancy dance, or a grass dance, or shawl dancing. For instance, nowadays we have a jingle dance; it's new and upcoming. You see that, too.

In creating a costume, one has to have an idea as to where the dance came from, where people learned the dance, who taught them that, or why they do certain steps, because in these dance contests we have judges. These judges are looking for something that's basic, authentic. So dancers go to a lot of trouble to put together their regalia and dancing, and learn the background.

The time of year when you hold a powwow matters, too. For instance, with the Ute Indians in Fort Duchesne, the powwow comes close to the Fourth of July. It's not really tied in with Independence Day, but it goes back to the old days when Indians used to participate in other doings around the Fourth of July—for instance, people went to rodeo.

It is also close to the summer solstice when the sun starts going to the south, and it may be a dance that's associated with that time. Certain ceremonies are tied in with the equinox, spring or fall, winter, and summer. The people had certain types of ceremonies that they performed. For instance, the Bear Dance may have been connected with something like that. It's the turning of season from one to another; maybe the stars are at certain levels.

The organization of powwow dancing itself is becoming a universal. The dance is really a dance that's been with the people for a long period of time. They didn't use the word powwow a hundred years ago; it's a new way of saying it. Not too long ago, maybe back about thirty to forty years ago, when someone said powwow, they meant a business meeting. Somewhere they were going to have a business meeting, hash it out, talk about certain things.

Powwow—that was a group of people getting together to talk about a certain issue. The word itself comes from back east, the name of a man in the eastern tribes. They would gather at his place, or his council, and they'd gather for a powwow. So the name was used by another group, and it went on and on and on, and now everybody uses it and it means dance.

You have a lot of words being used by all tribes that have no idea where the words originated. A silly word like "How"—you see that in the movies. No one knows who said that; I don't even know what tribe uses that. Then there's another word that goes around; Indian people use it a lot. They say, "A-ho. A-ho." For instance when I get through praying or talking, different tribes use that word, "A-ho." But when you go to another tribe, they use that, too. And somebody says that means, "All right, it's good." So then another tribe says the same thing—"Ah-o." And they describe it the same way—it means good. But what tribe really originated it? I don't know. Someone may know. It's impossible for all tribes to have the word and have it mean the same thing.

I guess what I'm getting at is this: We have the Uto-Aztecan-speaking people in this area, the Great Basin, the south, southwest. Then you have within that smaller groups, the Shoshonean speaking, the Numic speaking, then we have a breakdown of those groups, too. There are similarities in the way they say certain things. Then when you take the Algonquins over there—they're not the same. Then you take the Athabascans—they're not the same as the Algonquins or the Aztecan-speaking people. They're different.

So how could that word be the same for all of these? You've taken a tribe from the Algonquin group and one from the Uto-Aztecan-speaking group and both say "A-ho," and they say, "Well, that means 'good.'" Somewhere way back someone started using that word, and everyone said, "That's an Indian word." It's an Indian word all right, but it may belong to some tribe. Similarly, that's how the word pow-wow came into existence.

The way that people talk about it, when you go to powwow, you must always dance around clockwise—always. It's like a day; you travel with the sun as you dance. Each time you make a round, it makes one day from where you started. If you're sick, and dance around and come to that point again, you are one day out of sickness; you are ahead of it. You're always going away from your sickness; you are ahead of it. You're always going away from it when you go into the future, away from your sickness. If you dance counterclockwise, you are going back into your sickness again, your troubles again. You are wanting your sickness again, the troubles you had before. You like sickness, you like bad things.

The sun doesn't travel counterclockwise; it travels this way; so you have to go with it. Anyway, that's what I was taught, so that's why I dance this way. I haven't danced the opposite way yet; maybe I will. If somebody tells me why, and it sounds good, then I'll do it. But if it doesn't seem logical according to what I believe in a spiritual way, then I won't do it. It's got to be something that's stronger than how I believe.

If dancing counterclockwise is associated with something bad— if it had something to do with witching—then I don't think it's good to dance counterclockwise. People will say, "Well, that way, people won't witch you." That doesn't sound right. In the old days, hatred was there. The people didn't always look after each other in a good way. In certain families, that still exists, too.

The Indian way is really complicated in that way. Witching was something that could change your way of thinking, change you. Witching is like putting something in your mind; your mind then feeds to your blood; your blood then feeds to your body—it's bad.

For instance, if somebody says something bad to you, you catch it in your mind, and you think about it for so long that it begins to work on you, and it feeds into these other parts of your body. Your blood will carry it. You'll become sick. That's witching. So in order to purify that, you take a medicine man to clear up your mind again, so your mind allows a good spirit of God to go through your blood, into your body again, and heals you.

Most witching was deliberate; people did that. If they didn't like something, they'd rather see it dead. If they didn't like you, they'd rather see you dead. You have to deal with it. There were some things that happened without a cause, too, that were bad, so you might say, "Well, somebody did it," or "We did it; we didn't live right."

Indians have people who like to gamble; they get so involved in it, that's all they want to do. Medicine ways can be involved, too. They would go out and collect all these things they were going to use gambling. They'd finally get it all together and say, "I'm going to gamble." They'd win a lot of money.

If those people were living today, they would go to Las Vegas, Nevada. There's a way to do that—win at gambling. I saw a man do that—there are medicine ways.

My mother used to say, "I don't want you to sit by him, or sit in the same circle."

My dad talked about it, too. "Those things you have to watch for. If you use that power wrong, you're going to lose all your relatives, your kids. They're going to die off one by one. Eventually you're the one who's going to suffer. You're going to die a horrible death." That's what he said.

But anyway, I know what the secret was. It works that way, too. That's why I leave it alone.

I often wonder if in the Fremont or Anasazi cultures that the life was structured in such a way that their destruction was not something physical. I wonder if something in the way they thought, the way they lived, caused bad things and could cause them to vanish, too. You cannot find evidence anywhere, even if you look for it. The archaeologists do a lot of digging, analyzing, but they can't find the reason for their disappearance because it had no material or physical cause. It was something like a spiritual thing. It's the way they lived.

Somebody's got to study that because the life of those people was not how we live today. They didn't think like us. They didn't have a structure like ours. They died, they moved away, or they became a part of something else. Maybe they got swallowed up by an earthquake. Maybe there was an eclipse of the sun; maybe there was a change in atmosphere that made all of that happen. We don't know. Maybe there was a force beyond all description. Maybe they moved away. Maybe the big ship that brought them here came back, loaded them up, and took them back to where they came from. That ship may not be out there; it may be here.

I think this way: In this world that we live in, we are only living what we see. But in the same world, there may be another world. Right here may be another world. There might be a lot of people here, too. In the next world, maybe the whole country looks different in a way—another dimension. Maybe that's all it is. I think that way sometimes.

If you keep at a certain thing, you're going to find the answer within yourself. Which leads to only one thing: if you find the answer within yourself to a certain problem, that would mean that someone else lives within you—something else lives inside of you that is different than you. It tells you these things, so that's how you learn.

You know everything in this world to begin with; you know everything. You're born with the knowledge of everything about this world, and then as you go on to study in school, you are merely bringing it out. You are making a statue or an image out of yourself, to fit you, to become you. You already know the answer; you already know what you're learning; that's why it's easy. If it's hard—well, you're not trying hard enough; but you know the answer.

I could learn many things, too, if I put my mind to it. So that's why I think about spiritual things, like myself, like you; we have the same thing that's inside of us. The only different thing about you is that your outside color is white, and my outside color is dark.

How did I get on this subject? People dancing counterclockwise at powwows—they must believe in it. Or there must be insecurity, a feeling of insecurity. It could be, too, in a dance contest, that you think somebody's going to witch you and you're not going to win. So in order to avoid that you must dance this other way. That must be an insecure feeling for that individual.

If I'm going to win, I'm going to win. I'm going to win—nothing's going to stop me. If I'm going to be great, I'm going to be great. If you have a good feeling within yourself, nothing in this world is going to stop you. It's the way you block yourself as you go along— that's the only thing that's going to stop you. So people who dance counterclockwise must have a different teaching. They don't want to talk about it; nobody wants to talk about it. But I, myself, can't find the answer. There must be an answer, though, and I think it concerns witching, so people won't talk about it.

Even in ceremonies—Sun Dance ceremonies, teepee ceremonies—you always go to the left. You don't walk around backwards; people would laugh at you. I've seen backward dancing at other powwows. It's just the way people are. Eventually that will die out, though, I think.

I'm different at a powwow. Now I'm dressed like this: blue jeans, boots, cowboy hat. I enjoy myself like this in my everyday life, working, sometimes a little change here and there; sometimes I wear a necktie. It's always an impression that's coming from you to fit into the group that you're going to be meeting with, or talking to, or living with.

Then, being an Indian, you have a chance to change into another area when you go to powwow. Gradually you become a little different. Maybe you have a hair roach with a feather on top; maybe your face is painted; you have an Indian-pattern shirt, beaded, hair brushed into braids, wearing moccasins, carrying items you don't carry around in your everyday life.

Actually, you're not performing for the people. The people are watching you, but communication is in how you relate to each other by observing, participating. You are there knowing you are separate from the outside. You are expressing yourself in the Indian way. "Here's what I am. Here's what I think Indian is." Or, "Here's what I think my people were, and I'm still with it today. Those are not old items I'm wearing, they're new. I made them to dance in today.

If the language stays in the songs, that would be a way to preserve language, too. Most of us are oriented to English. The whole competition is based on English, based on European-type expressions. Everything that you do in America is really based on the European. We became that.

I speak English, but there's another side to me, too. Sometimes we bring those things out and talk Indian. But life has changed to the point where everything we do and everything we depend on is based on something that's on the white side. If you're going to feed your family, if you're going to provide for yourself, if you're going to become something, you've got to learn English and educate yourself. Nothing there is saying you've got to be an Indian; that's all foreign. And that's how we live.

So we keep the language, and sometimes we bring it out here, but mainly for show. Maybe we feel something missing, or some people say, "We want an Indian circle because that means more." So we bring it out. We say, "Let's try this thing; let's try that." But on the reservation, the Indian way of life stays in that one place. The language is there, too.

The language is important, but you weigh that with survival. A lot of people are caught in that thing; my kids are caught in that, too. They know what I'm talking about when I'm talking about a certain thing. But they'll ask, "What did they say in Ute when they said that?" Then they'll write it down.

My boy does that a lot. He writes Ute down the best that he can, then he tries to pronounce it. I tell him, "That's what I'm saying," or "That's what they were saying." He's a composer, too. He composes powwow songs and he inserts Ute words in them.

He comes to me and says, "How do you say this, Dad? How do you say, 'We're glad to see you. It's good to be here.'" He inserts the Ute words into the songs. They sing them at the powwows. Or, "I will see you again. I will see you sometime." So he keeps up with that. I feel good about it. At least he's preserving the words, and he's learning that way, too. That way he maintains the continuity.

I didn't really expect that out of him. I wanted him to stay on the path I followed. But then again, I performed, too, but not in the way he is. He's in the singing part, whereas I don't do the singing in a big powwow—I'm a dancer. But he does the singing. It gives him his own part. He's been doing that for several years.

Sunday, I asked him to come over to the house. I have a drum frame that I had one of my welder friends put together for me. He took a fifty-gallon drum and cut the end part, welded it together and made a frame. It's rounded so it's not going to cut anyone, but it's solid around the neck. I have three deer hides, and my son's going to take one and he's going to make a drum cover. I'm going to have a drum, and I'm going to use that to practice on. When I need one for dances or to show, I'm going to take that.

POWWOW

Fort Duchesne, Utah

Northern-style eagle feather bustle. Ute Intertribal Powwow, Fort Duchesne, Utah.

JULY 3, 1988

Clifford Duncan leading in the Grand Entry at the Ute Powwow, Fort Duchesne, Utah.

JULY 8, 1990

Clifford Duncan leading in the Grand Entry, carrying the Ute tribal flag. Ute Powwow, Fort Duchesne, Utah.

JULY 8, 1990

Men's Grass Dancer at the Ute Powwow, Fort Duchesne, Utah.

JULY 8, 1990

Men's Northern Traditional Style Bustle.

JULY 4, 1985

Northern Traditional Dancer with eagle feather bustle. Ute Intertribal Powwow,
Fort Duchesne, Utah.

JULY 6, 1990

Clifford Duncan with his friend Palmer Knowlden. The dancers are wearing Northern
Traditional-style regalia. Ute Intertribal Powwow, Fort Duchesne, Utah.

JULY 7, 1990

Northern Traditional Dancer with eagle feather bustle.
Ute Intertribal Powwow, Fort Duchesne, Utah.

JULY 8, 1990

Teen Northern Traditional Dancer. In background is Ryan Burson.
Ute Intertribal Powwow, Fort Duchesne, Utah.

JULY 8, 1990

Northern Traditional Dancer with medicine wheel beadwork on side-drop.
Ute Intertribal Powwow, Fort Duchesne, Utah.

JULY 8, 1990

Men's Grass Dancer. Ute Intertribal Powwow, Fort Duchesne, Utah.

JULY 8, 1990

Junior Boys Grass Dancer. Ute Intertribal Powwow, Fort Duchesne, Utah.

JULY 3, 1988

Men's Northern Traditional Dancer with beaded cuff.
Ute Intertribal Powwow, Fort Duchesne, Utah.

JULY 3, 1988

Clifford Jake, Paiute Elder with buffalo hat and large eagle fan.

Ute Intertribal Powwow, Fort Duchesne, Utah.

JULY 7, 1990

Palmer Knowlden, a friend of Clifford Duncan. Ute Intertribal Powwow, Fort Duchesne, Utah.

JULY 8, 1990

Northern Traditional Dancer with coyote hat.

JULY 4, 1985

"Baloo The Bear" (Eric Ridley), lead powwow singer and nephew of Clifford Duncan.

Ute Intertribal Powwow, Fort Duchesne, Utah.

JULY 6, 1991

Clifford Duncan. Ute Intertribal Powwow, Fort Duchesne, Utah.

JULY 6, 1991

Luke Duncan, Clifford Duncan's brother, on a Harley-Davidson. Ute Intertribal Powwow, Fort Duchesne, Utah.

JULY 3, 1988

Charlene Duncan in cloth wing dress. Ute Intertribal Powwow, Fort Duchesne, Utah.

JULY 6, 1991

Rena Duncan, Clifford Duncan's youngest child, waiting to dance.

Ute Intertribal Powwow, Fort Duchesne, Utah.

JULY 6, 1991

Teen Northern Traditional Dancers. Fort Duchesne, Utah.

JULY 7, 2008

Tiny Tot Dancers during Grand Entry. Ute Intertribal Powwow, Fort Duchesne, Utah.

JULY 9, 1990

Northern Traditional Dancer with eagle feather bustle carrying his dance stick.
Ute Intertribal Powwow, Fort Duchesne, Utah.

JULY 7, 1990

Clifford Duncan, on right, with his adopted uncle, Elwood Koshiway of the Comanche Tribe.
Grand Entry, Ute Powwow, Fort Duchesne, Utah.

JULY 8, 1990

Clifford Duncan in Southern Traditional regalia during Grand Entry at the
Fourth of July Ute Powwow, Fort Duchesne, Utah.

JULY 6, 2008

Grass Dancer. Fourth of July Ute Powwow, Fort Duchesne, Utah.

JULY 6, 2008

Theron Root (center) and Leroy Cesspooch (far left) in a cowboy hat along with other Drum Contest judges
at the Fourth of July Ute Powwow, Fort Duchesne, Utah.

JULY 6, 2008

Junior Girls Fancy Dancer. Ute Intertribal Powwow, Fort Duchesne, Utah.

JULY 3, 1988

Carolyn Boyer, Northern-style Buckskin Traditional Dancer.

JULY 4, 1985

Grass Dancer preparing to dance. Ute Intertribal Powwow, Fort Duchesne, Utah.

JULY 4, 1985

Ute Intertribal Powwow, Fort Duchesne, Utah.

JULY 8, 1990

"Retiring the colors." Ute Intertribal Powwow, Fort Duchesne, Utah.

JULY 4, 1985

Grass Dancer holding his child. Ute Intertribal Powwow, Fort Duchesne, Utah.

JULY 3, 1988

Clifford Duncan, dressed in Northern Traditional regalia and holding his eagle-wing fan.
Ute Intertribal Powwow, Fort Duchesne, Utah.

JULY 7, 1990

Fancy Dancers. Ute Intertribal Powwow, Fort Duchesne, Utah.

JULY 4, 1985

Fancy Dancer waiting for proper pickup of a dropped eagle feather.
Ute Powwow, Fort Duchesne, Utah.

JULY 4, 1985

Tiny Tot Traditional Dancer. Ute Intertribal Powwow, Fort Duchesne, Utah.

JULY 4, 1985

Lance Manning, Clifford Duncan's nephew, singing with his family drum group, Chepita Lake Singers.
Ute Powwow, Fort Duchesne, Utah.

JULY 4, 1985

Clifford Duncan enjoying the powwow with his family. Ute Intertribal Powwow, Fort Duchesne, Utah.

JULY 6, 1991

Women's Northern-style Traditional Dancers during Grand Entry.
Ute Intertribal Powwow, Fort Duchesne, Utah.

JULY 4, 1985

Woman Jingle Dancer during Grand Entry. Ute Intertribal Powwow, Fort Duchesne, Utah.

JULY 8, 1990

Northern Traditional Dancer. Ute Intertribal Powwow, Fort Duchesne, Utah.

JULY 4, 1985

Clifford Duncan, wearing a porcupine hair roach with a grouse feather visor and carrying an eagle-wing fan. Ute Intertribal Powwow, Fort Duchesne, Utah.

JULY 8, 1990

War Bonnet Dancer and Traditional Dancer leading in the Grand Entry with the American flag. Ute Intertribal Powwow, Fort Duchesne Utah.

JULY 4, 1985

This Man, Jesus

I refer to Christian ways at certain times. At certain times, I read the Bible—not all of it, but certain verses. What I'm looking for is in there. I then take that, and I interpret it into the way I think. This man, Jesus Christ, is not really what they think he is. When you do an in-depth study about the Bible or Christian ways, people actually are expressing how they look at it.

Therefore, if I go to the Catholic Church, the Episcopal Church, the Mormon Church, I begin to feel really alien because who they're talking about doesn't belong to me. People express belief in the way that belongs to them. If I tell you something, it is coming from me— only me; you are an alien. That is wrong; you are not alien, but you have to put my expression into words that fit your life.

This man, Jesus, was an indigenous person. To me, he was indigenous because what he learned were the traditional ways of the old people, not today's ways. They had no television in those days, no cars. So why do we talk about it as if the world was modern? He didn't speak in a way that sounded poetic or with the spiritual level tied in. Scripture is the way this person wrote. Christianity and Indian religion are not oil and water any more. They have become one thing. One of my old friends from Rocky Boy, Montana, an elder the same age as my father or older—he made friends with my dad many years ago when I was a boy, so I think of him as a father—he would tell me things when I would visit him. We'd sit down and talk; and he'd talk, and talk, and talk, and tell me about different things in this world, from his viewpoint.

So one day he said, "These people, the white people, talk about Jesus Christ. I had a good talk with the minister, and we discussed a lot of things. I told him about our stories. You know those stories, Clifford—stories about Coyote, the trickster, the Badger, the Buffalo, and the Snake, and how the winters come when the northern geese bring the northern winds across this land.

"We were brought up that way; we learned this; we relate to these things, how the world's going to be. The animals and birds created this world for us. They taught us how to talk, taught us how to sing, showed us how to dance, all of that.

"Then there was one man who was really powerful. He could do good; he could do bad; but he was a magician. In a simple way, we say it that way. I come to this conclusion that the Bible and the so-called mythology we talk about—our stories—are equivalent to each other. It's the way we interpret it. Jesus was a man who did what these animals did, too. This animal did the same thing he did; so they're parallel. The levels of the creation stories are the same height, nothing lower, nothing higher. So when you look at the old way of life today, even though it's an Indian way, we have to keep looking at the Christian side, because there are similarities." That's what he would tell me.

You could find in the Sun Dance, for instance, things occurring that could be interpreted in the Christian way. You could say, "This is the center; the center is God. All things are going toward the center. The poles go from the sides to the center; that's your god. The circle represents the world; God made this world. On all the different edges of the world, there are different kinds of people. So God created the world. The light comes up in the morning. God created light: '"Let there be light."'

In the Indian way then, you take the Sun Dance again: The Sun Dance is really you; it is who you are within yourself; then you are looking at yourself as the center. The center Sun Dance pole is really the inner core of your life, your spirit that's placed within your body at the time of birth. It has all the answers.

When you were born into this world, God gave you everything. All the tools you need to survive were given to you and placed within this little cylinder within you. You are the only one who has a key. Or some people put it this way: the door only opens from one side. No outside person can open it because the doorknob is only built so that you can open it. If you open the door, all things will come in. Otherwise, if people talk to you and try to open that door, they can never do it. That's the way the world is made; your body, your spirit, is created that way.

So the Sun Dance represents you. You are the one that's going to go down and touch the center part—the center pole—and talk to it. You are actually talking to yourself. You have all the answers within yourself. So when you do spiritual work within the Sun Dance, the sweat lodge, or the other ceremonies, you will find most of the answers within you. You're going to find it and say, "*I have it.*" Or you're going to listen to yourself—as you talk; listen, because you're going to be talking to yourself. In the talk itself, you're going to find the answers given to you. So the Sun Dance represents that, too.

So you look at it two ways. In a Christian way, there are teachings that we have from the outside that center on Christ or God. If you look at it from the Indian way, it is your life; it's you; you're the one who has control of everything within yourself and around you. That's where it is.

In the Native American Church, we say we're going to take it in a Christian way. Here we talk to Jesus. Still, it's different in that in a white man's church, you talk *about* Jesus, you talk *about* God—it's a theology. In this religion, we talk *to* God.

I was thinking about that some time ago, thinking about things in a different way. What I'm doing is I'm talking to God; I'm talking to the creator of this world; I'm talking to the force that makes all things what they are. There has to be a force in almost anything we do—energy—you name it. Each energy then takes its form—a tree, a plant. Each becomes what it is. Animals, the same way—they become animals; birds become birds.

The spirit is invisible. The force is invisible. The energy is invisible. But it has to be somewhere around us, so close that we inhale it; it goes in with the air, then comes back out as something else. It goes in each person through the water, through the air, or through the ceremony. So everything is then powered; it's a spiritual power around us.

You address that in a different way. You don't say, "Spirit, you…" You don't say it that way. You say, "Spirit, power, or *puwa*—you are there, and you created things."

So we have all these things, as if each one has a brand name on it. Here's a Sony. You fix it, but you use only the parts that fit a Sony. Here's a Chevrolet. You get the parts that fit only that machine. The same with everything you do—a computer has a brand name on it; only certain parts fit it. Everything's there. You don't take anything different from what it's intended to be.

So you are talking to the creator. "Okay," you say, "you made us; you made me. You know what goes into this." It's not really asking or telling, but it's saying something. Then you, because you are powerful (you don't do anything without a thought behind it—you've got to think it out, get it right), you make an adjustment to correct all things around this, and it becomes whole. The person becomes well because you put all the right parts into that person.

You are that. Then you are so small that I can pick you up. Then you are so big, this world is yours—you made the universe. We're not talking about size; we're not talking about weight; we're not talking about limitation of power; we're not talking about expansion of power. We're talking about something that's the center of all that. The center is where the whole thing started. You can't catch it—it's so small, so big.

My relationship with *that*, as a person, is different. I am inside of it now. I am inside of the creation, safe inside the center of the thought origin. My relationship with God is that way. I have put aside the idea that someday I will leave God because I never will. I'm already inside of him, and already around him; or he's around me. That's my relationship with him.

It is the same way with other spirits; Christ is the same way, too. The meditation process touches a little bit on that. So your Christ, our Christ in the Christian way, is there.

One night I was in a ceremony with this old man—he died several years ago, a Cheyenne, married to one of my aunts; they're both gone. They went to peyote meetings a lot. I'd see them there. This man was about eighty-five. The meeting would be sponsored by somebody else. We were just there because we heard about it. Somebody else was conducting the meeting.

Once in a while this old man would get to the point where he wanted to tell me something. Without thinking about anything else, but without being disrespectful, he would bring it up because it was there. He would be sitting on this side or that side, but I would be sitting on the opposite side.

When the drum stopped, he would say, "Clifford. I'd like to tell you something."

So I said, "Thank you." Everything would stop.

He did that one time. He said, "Clifford, Jesus Christ is *your* personal savior." That's what he said. My wife and the others listened to him. "He belongs to *you*," he said, "the way that you are using him. Don't listen to anybody else as to what Jesus is, or what he can do, or what he can't do. If somebody sees him in another way, that's his—this is yours, and you are his."

So when he talked to me and said, "Jesus Christ is *your* personal savior," all these people kind of laughed. The man watching the fire put cedar on to sanctify his statement, make it solid.

People would say, "He's not talking to us. He's talking to him." They took it that way. "He's not telling us that. He was telling him." Then they'd laugh. "Why doesn't he talk to all of us?" "No, he wants to talk to him. That's why he used his name."

So once in a while, this old man would do that. One time he said, "Clifford, you're going into this world. Indian ceremony—what's going on here—Indian ceremony is your shield. You hold your shield high in your hand. All things that are coming toward you will bounce off. When you go out into the world, hold that shield up high. You must remember that. The ceremonies that you have, you hold up. It's where you're coming from. That's the only thing that's going to protect you, because you don't have anything else."

In a way that's true, because you have to have a place that you come from, things that you learn, certain beliefs—you're coming from there. So our relationship with God or spiritual things is oriented toward people in the past who lived life a little different than ours, and it goes back and back and back into history. To learn, you go and listen to them—a group of people who have never been exposed to television or radio; they are in buckskins. They don't know anything beyond what they know. But they know enjoyment; they know pleasure and difficulty only within that. Music is the same way, the songs.

I have another friend, who's sick now. He went to Jerusalem for about six weeks; he just returned two weeks ago. I talk to him a lot. I listen to him talk. Over there, they were talking about how to steal things—how these groups here and there are different in certain ways. The Palestinians are like the Indian tribes. They're way back on this side. They remind him of Indian tribes.

That goes back to how I think about those things. You go back two thousand years. Here's Jesus, or maybe he had another name. He was the son of a carpenter. Joseph was a carpenter. When you use the word carpenter, he's the one with a saw, hammers, nails, a square, building a house like this. That's a carpenter the way we look at it today. Maybe then that was a word that they used to describe something else—maybe a handyman, or maybe he worked here and there.

The people then were Indians, Indian-like, small groups of people here and there. They sat on the floor, ate on the floor, and they had a family structure that is different here, now. Only certain ones could do certain things. So their thinking was different than we imagine it. When you read the Bible, you read in between the lines, not what's in print. There's a message going on in between the lines, and it's up to you to read it and make out the meaning. That's where you find the difference.

They had a funeral down here some time ago, a grandmother of mine. The Episcopal priest was presiding over that. One of our daughters was there. The priest was standing there in a brown outfit, white hair. This child is standing there as the people pass by, viewing the body.

The child said to the priest, "You're not God."

The priest says, "Oh?"

"And you're not Jesus. Jesus is not white like you. Your ancestors are different, too. He did not look like you."

"Oh? I'd better stick around here. I might learn something from you," the priest told her.

I think of it in the way that this man, Jesus, was like any person that grew up in a home that had nothing. How would you be if, from the day that you're born, they took you away and put you with a Navajo family in a hogan? You would accept things as you went along, as a way of life. If they gave you a tortilla-like bread, you'd accept that—it's bread. Then if you go out of there some years later, and they give you a loaf of bread, you'll say, "No, that's not bread."

So this man grew up a certain way and that's the way he was. He lived a certain life in his earlier years that made him what he was as an adult. But they talk about only what's up front; they don't talk about how he grew up, or where he grew up. Everything there is put away because they want to talk about his miracles and interpret them in the way they can distribute Christianity throughout the world. You don't hear anything of his boyhood.

He became a great magician or *puwaghat*. I believe that. There's a man named Campbell, Joseph Campbell. He wrote a book called, *The Hero with a Thousand Faces*. I have that book, but I haven't had time to read it. One day I'm going to sit down and read it.

The book is based on that simple thing, that prophets were not limited to a certain group; they were all over, everywhere in this world. The power of these people was felt throughout the world. Jesus was one of them. But they would teach each other, too; the power went on and on. Let me give you an example on the Indian side.

One thing that we, as Indian people, sometimes look at is this: I was talking to a Navajo boy one day. He told me about his brother, how he got an eagle feather from a live bird, and later he'd gotten sick. This Navajo boy wanted me to run a meeting for his brother, but he wanted me to go down there. I told him I would do it here. That way I know what I'm doing. I don't want any interference from any other way of life or belief. I know the Navajos have their own beliefs, and I respect them. They're going to interfere with me when I'm in Navajo country because a lot of people are going to watch me. I don't want that.

If I'm going to do something for him, I want to do it at my house. I will do it with my people because they know me. That way, everything I do goes toward his boy, with no interference from the side.

I talked with him later on, and he said, "We went ahead and arranged a ceremony down here."

I said, "That's fine. But I'd like to tell you something over the phone. The way I look at it, how it's going to work: I'm going to be visiting several places between now and tomorrow evening, on the reservation. These are places where I have done a lot of spiritual work by myself. I'm going to put tobacco here, a certain thing there, a prayer here; it's going to bring these back to life—for you."

I don't believe in the idea that only one man can bring healing. I believe in the idea that it takes several to make things complete. So, thinking my way, you don't say, "I did it." Everybody did it. Everybody was part of this process of healing.

I told him, "When I do that, I would like for you to tell your people there is no distance. We think that I have to be *there*. In my way of thinking, I will be there with him, and he will be here with me, so we will sit side by side. We are traveling over the world at the speed of light; so I will listen to him and he will listen to me. You have to put aside this other thing, that there is distance."

I will call someone who is clear down on the other side, maybe in Oklahoma. I will tell him what's happening here, and he will say, "Hey, it's happening down here." But he doesn't know where that came from—or maybe he does, because his mind is open. There is a spaced area that goes from here to there. If I can find that area, I will shoot this—from here to there—and it will reach him. In a spiritual way, that's how you think. An arrowhead will pierce the skin. So we use that image in a spiritual way to say, "I will shoot this to him."

The sunrise has arrows that pierce the sky. The first sun ray that comes over the mountains shoots out. You have to be careful where you're standing. So that's how we believe as spiritual people.

That would mean that in the old days, back there in the time of Christ, they were communicating that spiritual way with people elsewhere, such as in the Far East. So Jesus could be taught that way. If everybody believed that way, that was the way it would be. Everybody, the community as a whole, the eastern part of the world, believed in certain ways at that time; so it was easy for them to communicate mentally. Nowadays it's different. Even though we are all together, we are not together. So that's the way that was.

Jesus, now, is the only one we know about because these others; if you don't write about them or keep records, they are lost. Actually, they are not lost, they're still there. But this one, Jesus, happens to be the one that's widely known.

So in the way I say it, the power that's here, the prophets of the past, their ways of thinking, have been placed in order somewhere,

here or there. But we have taken Jesus to represent all. He represents all the power of all those who contributed to spiritual ways. So in our way of thinking, Jesus is holding on to some of the things that are Indian, too.

You're going to look at it in a Christian way. You could use some other image; that could fit, too. That would depend entirely on you.

26

Culture Clash

Recently a counselor asked me, "Why do some Indians say that they don't like being Indian? They would rather be a white person. Why do they say that?" Young people had been saying that to this young man who had been working with the Indian kids in a trade school sponsored by the Episcopal Church.

I hit on a few things trying to find an answer: maybe they don't know what it is to be an Indian because they have nothing to draw from. They don't know where they're coming from because that's how they grew up. Maybe the whole family's that way. They don't know the inside of what is really good about Indian life. That's how I answered that.

If I go to an Indian ceremony, the thing that I want from it is the spiritual contact. I've lived in the way that I'm oriented to what the experience will be like, or what it means. So I'm deriving that, and I experience that.

Then there are Indian families that haven't been exposed to that; they talk against it. They don't want it; they don't like it. I would think to myself this way: I'm glad they don't want it, because that way they won't bother it. So I can have it because I know. I feel sorry for them because they don't know what they're talking about. If they only knew that there is something there besides what we see. They don't go into the Indian thinking regarding whatever is there.

I would say that seventy-five percent of the Indian people are on the side of assimilation. Very few are actually what you'd consider traditional. I don't know how the modern Indian culture would be described.

I was in church one day—my grandchildren were baptized in the Episcopal Church. That's where I grew up, around there. My mother used to go to the Episcopal Church. We used to walk a mile just to go to church. We didn't have a car. Afterward, we'd have a sandwich, coffee, and a social gathering; we would talk, sit around, and read magazines. They had a lot of magazines they'd bring in, and there were a lot of people there when I was a boy. But at this baptismal of my grandchildren, there were only a few in the congregation. It made me sad because I used to see a full church.

Then I start thinking about other things—Indian ways, traditional ways. There is a wide gap in between the traditional way and the non-Indian way. We are saying, "Live the old traditional way of thinking," to our people, to our children. You hear a lot of people talk about that, a lot of comments. When you take a good look at it, from where I sit, the old Indian traditional culture is way out there, far from us, and the dominant American culture is way on this side. There's a big empty space in between. What we have to do is bring the old ways as close as possible to the center. Then by getting the two sides married off, you will have an offspring. The offspring will be half and half, a touch of both. These two ways of life have not gotten married yet; they're not even engaged yet.

We talk about Indian ways—you talk to a group of kids and tell them, "Don't drink. If you are drinking, get help. Don't go to that counseling program. Go see a medicine man."

Yet this adolescent is not going to do that because the way of the medicine man is way out there—the two sides haven't gotten engaged yet. This young person is in the gap, looking for tradition because somebody tells him, "The Indian way is good for you." But he doesn't want to walk way over to reach the medicine man. The white way is so easy because it's closer—you just drive over there. This medicine man is sitting up too high; you don't want to climb there.

Besides, this young person says, "I'm not Indian. I don't want to be Ute. I'm ashamed of being Indian." A girl said that. "I'm ashamed of being Indian." It shouldn't be that way, but it's there.

I was thinking about that. At the same time, I realized that within this church service, they had this bread and wine ritual. So my wife and daughter went up to the front and knelt down. But they know I don't do that. The reason I don't do that is because I'm not a member of the Episcopal Church. I was never baptized in any Christian church, in fact. I'm the only one in the family who wasn't. So in my way of thinking, I am not Episcopalian even though I believe in their ways of doing things, and I respect them. I'm Christian because I've been to different churches, and I know how they pray. I learned the Christian ways. I grew up that way; I'm a Christian, but I don't belong to them. They don't belong to me; I'm neutral and we understand each other.

When I go to the Indian ceremony, I see Christian concepts in there, too. It's my personal way of doing things. I believe in my way because I'm brought up this way. I believe in Jesus Christ. I believe Christianity. I also believe that this other thing, which I call the Indian way, is not really the old way.

If you come to me and you tell me, "I want to do rituals in the old Indian way," I'm caught in the middle. I've been praying this way, and I believe this Christian way too; so I don't know what to tell you.

Maybe I put the Christian part away and I tell you only the Indian part. "This represents the Holy Spirit, the spirit of the pine trees, the spirit of the waterfall, the spirit of the bird in flight." I give you a poetic description of how things work. "God created us; we came riding on a big turtle"—all of that. "You've got to hold your pipe this way; make an offering to the Holy Spirit; wear your blanket this way; wear your moccasins—this design means that; these feathers are going to do certain things for you." All of that—there are a lot of ways you could explain that.

Sitting over here is that other thing—Christianity—which talks about the same thing described over here. But maybe you want to say it in the traditional way so this newcomer, who is looking for what is Indian, will see what you're doing as traditional.

The other thing is this: white people are gullible. I'm going to start charging you after a while for something on the Indian side, so that's why I'm saying it traditionally. If I mention Jesus Christ to you, you're going to walk away from me. Maybe I'm reaching for your pocketbook, or I'm reaching for something else that you're going to give to me willingly. That happens sometimes.

I find that Indian people today have problems that they have actually picked up from the white side—for instance, a lot of alcohol problems. They are trying to find a solution from the same place where they got the problem. The answer might be on the other side. I think it's going to be a simple thing, too, once they find it. It's all a matter of discipline. You are the one—discipline. People treat alcoholism like a sickness—okay, true. But sickness is only a name given to that, not a solution for it. It's merely a description; that's all it is. Symptoms, they say, a sickness. Someone once said you cannot solve a problem with the same mind that created it.

I think I reached my conclusion this way. When I was a young man, I used to smoke cigarettes, a lot of cigarettes. I smoked about two packs a day. That's before I went into the army. Camels, I liked Camels—they make you dizzy. You kind of stagger around a little bit. That's what I liked; I got a kick out of it, you know. You look cute, too, hanging around outside, the cigarette dangling from your lip. Pull it out, inhale it, make the smoke come out of your nose. You say to the other person, "Watch, I'm going to make it come out of my ears." Then you stick the cigarette out to the side a little, burn them.

The person says, "Oh! You burned me."

You say, "No! You just saw smoke come out of my ears."

Anyway, you kind of a cough a little bit because the tobacco is in your system.

I went in the army. After a few weeks, going out to the field, marching here and marching there, five miles out to the rifle range, twenty miles up the hill, overnight hiking, all of that, I couldn't hack it. So in desperation, I said, "Well, it might be this cigarette that's doing it to me. I think I'll quit." I threw my cigarette away. That was it. I quit—in one day.

When I got back from the service, I'd drink beer, get drunk—that was the same way. You have different kinds of drinks. The other person orders something else. You say, "What's that? Let me try it. Oh, that tastes better than this." You drink for social reasons; you're mixing with the crowd. You pick up a boyfriend or girlfriend; sometimes you get into a fight, too. So all of this is in the center of drinking. You don't pay attention to it—you don't know what's going on—only that you're enjoying yourself. That's the way the world was for me.

So you incorporate drinking into your real life. You bring your beer home and put it in your refrigerator to keep it cool. "I'll have a beer once a day." It becomes a normal, everyday thing for an average American. You see commercials where they sit down and drink beer, so you're like that, too—you're going to be like the rest of the world! But, you know, on the other side, there's something else, too. You can get drunk. You can't have one or two; you've got to have four, got to have five. Then you say, "Let's go get a case. Let's go to somebody's house."

Then you begin to think about how all of these things happen in your life; it's the people that you associate with that are pulling you. You follow the crowd. So one day you say, "Well, I'm going to quit doing this," and everybody gets mad at you. All at once, you have enemies. All at once, you're not popular any more. You're alone, you're by yourself. When you say, "I'm going to quit. I'm going to quit going with you fellows because I'm getting in trouble," you find yourself alone, and that is what you were afraid of all the time. You don't know how it is to be lonely, yet loneliness can be the beginning of another life—and that's what people fear.

At the same time, loneliness has to accept another element that's going to be close to it, and that's discipline. So you have now picked up another person, and his name is discipline. A lonely person with a good discipline can go a long ways. Then as time goes on, this discipline will tell you, "One day, they'll come back to you. They'll talk to you."

So you see that one day, too. "Hi, brother. How have you been?"

"Oh, pretty good. You?"

"Oh, doing all right."

However, he doesn't say anything about drinking. They all have accepted you as a person who changed. That's how you get out of it. One day, you just do it. One day, you changed and said *no*. The thing that helped you through the change was discipline, but you knew that you were going to be alone.

People are afraid to be alone. I guess the whole world's that way. We are afraid of the darkness. We are afraid of being alone. We are the type of creature that needs others to make us what we are. We follow the others.

If the world one day says, "All women will have bald heads. They will have their hair shaved off because that's fashionable," everybody will do it. They read magazines that show you how to dress, what to buy. Every fall they say, "School shopping." There's no need to school shop because you already have clothes. But the world says "school shopping," so everybody goes. People like to be controlled; they like someone to follow. So that happens.

It's this world that we live in, a world of creativity. If I keep talking to you, eventually you will learn to think in a different way, rather than think in the way you were born with. You're born into this world, and you are never taught how to think. If you touch the stove, you pull back. That's hot. Then you don't touch it again because you know what happened. But nowadays people are coming up with so many ideas, they hold seminars to teach you how to be a certain way—how to think like a millionaire, how to think like an executive, how to make good speeches. It's all based on how to think and how to talk. It goes on every day. People make money on it. So eventually you're lost.

At the same time, you deal with a lot of laws. When I was growing up, my dad and my mother—if there was something wrong that I did, or we did as a group—they would take the strap to us. It hurt! We were punished that way. We would cry, it hurt. But we knew why they did it. Sometimes it was severe, sometimes mild. But they never sat us down to talk to us.

So as time went on, thinking about the whole thing, how I live and how I see people live, I say, "That was the best thing that ever happened to me because I knew at a young age how things should be." I was brought up that way. I like it. I don't go for this idea of just talking to your kids—the theory that you don't punish them, don't spank them. That is really ruining our people, our way of life.

I look at it this way: the young kids, they know what the laws are. So they do things and say, "Well, you can't spank me. That's child abuse." They hide behind these things, and before you know it they're adults and they're not really controlled. So you have a lot of problems and a lot of bad things going on because of the way they grew up. They don't know how it feels to be punished.

One has to recognize that true abuse goes beyond discipline, because to discipline is to teach. An elephant trainer trains the elephant at a young age. They tie a small chain around their feet, then put it on a little peg in the ground. A small elephant can't pull the peg out. All their lives, that's how they tie them up. When they're old, they're powerful, but that small peg still holds them. They believe they can't pull it out. They're trained. They're very useful; they can do a lot of things.

The main thing in life centers around how you discipline yourself. If you have a discipline within yourself, you can do anything you want in this world. Discipline is merely controlling yourself. You go into a classroom and sit down, and you discipline your mind to learn. If you don't have that, you're going to have a hard time in school. Going beyond that, ceremony is discipline; that's all it is. There's nothing hard about ceremony. It's how you look at it. The more discipline you have, the more your advantage, the better you are. Some people have it but not to the point where they live it. We all are a little like that. That's how I look at it.

Disciplining children has another meaning to me, rather than hurting. Discipline has nothing to do with abuse. Somehow it's gotten out of control. We've become prisoners of our own selves.

You take the Fremont people. If you think back, the life pattern is totally different than how we live. The center of it is totally different than how we live, passed on from generation to generation at different levels. We live at a different level than they did, and when we interpret from our level, we interpret their lives incorrectly. The archeologist is at a different level. We're all at different levels. A touch of that ancient level is within all ceremonies. But it's up to us to find it.

Religion, God, and ceremonies are a frontier we need to rediscover. We have to make a full turn and go back into it, try to find the true meaning of why we do the things we do. We lost the contact because we keep following this other road. For instance, we join a church. Then, over here, we stand on the stage someplace and say, "I'm an American Indian, and I believe this way." That person doesn't know a damn thing about Indian religion. (Excuse my language.) He's wrong. He doesn't understand.

For instance, Brigham Young University has a group of young people that entertain—they call themselves the Lamanite Generation. If it were at all possible, and the ancient people were brought here and somebody told them what was going on, they would laugh. "What are they doing? What is he talking about? No, he's a white man."

We have become a race within a race, a race away from our own race, by accepting this other life. We are somewhat invisible, yet unrecognized; there is still something that makes us different. We are going through a struggle. People sometimes refer to it as culture clash.

Culture clash began when the Europeans stepped on this continent, and we still have it today. Some of us are aware of different levels. When I say that maybe one day, I would like to build a cabin with a dirt floor, what I am saying is that I would like to turn around. That doesn't mean I am going to be different from other people, but I'm going to take this life and push it back into this ancient way because the answer is in our past. That's how we look at the world in a spiritual way—the answer is not up front. You have to find it in the back. Then once you find the answer, you bring it forward all the way to the front.

Native Americans are made to think that we are defeated. The country was taken away from us through a process now believed among us to be a defeat. On the other side we are saying, "No, we were not defeated. They cheated us. They took the land away from us." We have a cold war that goes on all the time, losing a sense of reality about what really happened, an outcome of the so-called doctrine of discovery.

I believe this: everything in this world has a physical and a spiritual element to it. When you give a gift, it isn't a gift until your spirit gives it, too. Native Americans never gave away this land. It was taken from us, but we didn't give it. On a physical level, Americans own the land. But on a spiritual level, the way I look at it, the country still belongs to Native Americans.

For instance, if you are forced away from here, you're going to think, "Well, I didn't leave it on my own, so I left part of myself here." When the Utes moved from Colorado to Utah, we left part of us there. There's no way anyone can change that because it isn't visible. You can't erase that. Even a congressional act is not going to erase it. It's just there. That's how I look it.

Somewhere in Europe began a change in the civilization. People refer to it as linear thinking. Linear thinking, over the centuries, became our legacy today. Americans place linear thinking up front. It's based on a simple thing.

When I get up on a stage, I make sure I'm higher up, so I look down at the people. People watch me. I say whatever I want. The impression developed is the sense that I know more than they do. They're all looking upward to learn something from me. That's how they're going to live, so I am the ruler.

We're set up the same way in the tribal council. There are six people that make the laws, but that way of doing things comes from the other side of the ocean. Native Americans have picked it up. It's not the Indian way because the Indian way is a little different. There was nobody out front. There was a great big circle and everybody sat side by side all the way around, no beginning and no end. Nobody sat out front; everybody had a chance to talk. It was a communal way of life, which was tied in with a spiritual way of life for everyone. That's how it worked.

Then the European side and the Indian side came together creating something new. That's why I say we must turn around and go back to find the answer. The answer is not in the lifestyle we've adopted today.

Let's put it this way: Indians are not the only victims. I see a lot of white people hurt, too. Somehow the American lifestyle doesn't work for them either. The American way of thinking is based on the idea that you are going to lose something as you go along. The weak will drop out; the strong will survive. That's how the Darwinian theory of how that works.

We have to somehow go back to a way of worship, a way of life, that still maintains that all are equal. That's where it is. The old Indian way is still there; we have to develop our thinking from that direction.

So, what we do is send our kids to school—educate them. Educate them to what? The European way, which was brought from over the sea, dominates all classrooms. Actually, our children are being led back into the same loop. Why don't we educate them to this other thing?—because it will conflict with the majority of thinking. As a result, this one gains; this one loses.

Some of my people that go to ceremonies, the old ones, they are getting on this linear side, but they still talk about spiritual things. They do this so that they'll be recognized, or they will get money out of it. White people are so gullible in the way they accept Indian ways. The Indian knows that. So he goes over here and tells them something. Before you know it, he's married to one of them, or he's getting money to do something. Other Indian people say, "Hey, that's wrong."

They answer, "No, it's not because it's open to everybody." Everybody belongs to the spirit; everybody belongs to God; but it's the system that makes it different. It's not that spiritual living is coming from both sides. Indian religion is not coming from the European way of thinking; it's coming from over here. It's not a solid triangle—there's a weak line somewhere. There's a strong line coming from the old Indian ways, but the spiritual line coming from Europe is weak. I think it's the way the Europeans interpreted their world because they adopted linear thinking with a purpose in mind—that eventually they would control the world. That's where they went wrong. That type of thinking can destroy the world.

Science and Religion

In the ceremonies we do, if you are a student of that type of religion or belief you find that it exists everywhere. At one point I spoke on a program for the Utah Rock Art Association. Afterward a man came up to me and said, "I've been thinking about asking you a question. I've always been after you, and I want to ask you something. I went to a Sun Dance once, and I had a friend who went to someplace in the Far East—Tibet, someplace like that. This man had picked up some dirt and sprinkled it around. My friend asked him, 'Why do you do that?' It was part of the ritual. He answered, 'I don't know, but I do it.'"

He continued, "Then, when I was watching the people at the Sun Dance, they sprinkled dirt over their feathers, and they sprinkled dirt on people, too. I wondered why. Why is it that a tradition on the other side of the world you do over here, too?" He wanted to ask me that.

I said, "Well, I'll talk to you about what I think about it. There are several answers, but I will give you one. When there's a sick person or someone who's not feeling well, we pray for that person. We all know that we are made up of things that we eat that come from Mother Earth. That's our life; she feeds us. She will give us things if you ask in the right way. If you perform a ritual that will make the right connections, it's going to come from her, too. So we're asking our mother to make us whole again. We sprinkle the spirit of our mother over the body to touch our mind, head, body, down to our feet. The spirit of the Mother Earth goes into us. We are blessing ourselves with our mother. Our mother is talking to us. That's why we do that. It has a power to heal; that's where the power is."

If you take that line of thought a little bit further, a man told me this: for certain sicknesses, you wet the dirt. Put water on it, or some saliva on it, to wet it. Then you talk to it, put it in your mouth, swallow it. That's how you do it. But it has to be part of a ritual. You don't just eat it. This treatment is for certain types of sicknesses; you have to know what it's for. It comes from Mother Earth.

So that's what I said to this man. Also, you give earth to the four directions. You always have to give to your constituents, followers, leaders, or teachers. The world is for everybody; it has a lifetime that is longer than ours. The life span of the world is millions of years old, and it has millions of years to go before it will finally die. God made it that way.

Therefore it is wrong for people to do things, to create things that destroy some of the atmosphere—they are shortening the life of the earth. It is wrong to make marks on the world—like taking a whole mountain down, tearing it up, putting it someplace else. You are scarring the world. You are shortening the life of the planet. It should be left alone. Don't be defacing or damaging the surface of the world; you are changing the process. Everything you do changes something, somewhat; everything is all tied together.

Last night, that's one of the things I was talking about. Even though all things are separate, such as a tree, grass, water, we are all put together by this invisible force. We're not actually related as a brother, but all things are tied in. Because the earth is in you, you're not separate from it, yet it's the whole thing. You're not separate, yet you're separated; related yet not related; all connected. That's how the world is.

By destroying one thing, you are destroying yourself. By destroying a culture, you are destroying yourself. By destroying a group of people over there, you are destroying yourself. You think that you are doing it to get rid of them, but you are destroying yourself, too.

It's good to have money coming from the resources taken from the earth. You're happy; you live better—as when we take oil out of the ground. But you have to think about the fact that there's nothing there after you take the oil out. What does that do to the Earth? Does it have some kind of effect that happens because it is empty there? You're throwing it off balance. Over billions of years the Earth became balanced, so the weights were equally distributed. If you take part of it, it's lopsided. It's going to get worse. So you have to think about it that way.

Disturbing under the surface of the earth, if you have a big bomb, the bomb contains a lot of things that are not coming from one place but from various places around the world. Actually there's a big hole there under the Earth's crust. Something's got to come from somewhere to fill that back up again. So over here, the earth drops—you have an earthquake.

You have disturbances on the surface, too, such as hurricanes. Strong winds are determined by what is not there—space that doesn't have an adequate amount of air, so the wind rushes in and fills that up. It makes it easier for air to shoot out because there's nothing there. When the wind is strong, it's telling you something, that somewhere there is something wrong.

We're actually destroying ourselves and the balancing of the world by doing these things. That's what I think.

I think one has to object to things. In your life you have to object; you can't go on as if everything is okay. Going back to this linear way of thinking, white people tend to think this way. People are trained from the time they go to school on the first day to accept only things that can be proven scientifically. That's the way we are. That's how far our thought goes. If it can't be proven, you don't believe it.

You have to, in your life, come to the point where you object to that. And that's where the Indian or spiritual way of thinking comes in. I believe in things that I do not see, things beyond seeing. Objecting to a concrete view of the world actually is a key to opening your mind to what's possible. You have to be like that. You have to think there are things out there that are really unexplored.

Sometimes I'm with archeologists out in the field. Sometimes we look at Fremont pictographs and petroglyphs. The Anasazi have their own; they have a meaning that is a little different than the way scientists look at it. Archeologists are really picturing what they see according to a system they have learned; it's all systemized as to which drawing means a certain thing. They have books written, and once it's printed it is supposed to be some kind of authority. They may not even know anything about it, but people will say, "The book says that."

A couple of months ago I went to Moab. A lady archeologist had called and wanted someone to go down and check the pictographs down in Sego Canyon, north of Thompson, an old mining town. So I went down there and met her at the junction. We took her four-wheel drive and went to Thompson and then into the upper country.

We checked out the one big area she was talking about, pictographs and petroglyphs on the wall, a panel of them. While we were there, several cars from out of state pulled up. They knew about these panels. That's why the archeologists had suggested fencing the area so there would be no disturbances because people were vandalizing various areas. They wanted me to check it out and give some advice as to what I think about this as an Indian person, what the pictographs mean to me.

Well, I looked at those panels from a religious point of view. Whenever I come into these issues, I try to analyze it in a spiritual manner. As time went by, finally I had to ask her this question because it was bothering me: "Do you believe in God?"

She said, "No, I don't believe in any church. I look at the world differently."

Within myself I thought, it's no use talking to her. What was she doing here, studying these things? I was wondering why she studies these things, which talk about religion, about God? She doesn't understand them because she doesn't accept it. She was facing these pictographs blind. If I tried to tell her, tried to talk to her, she still would not understand. That's really the way she is, the way she says she is. You have to believe in it from the beginning in order to understand. I cannot make someone believe in God.

I really don't know what made me ask her that. I don't go around asking anybody that. Something was there that made me ask. Maybe it was the panels. I had a pouch of tobacco. Every time we would go to another panel, I would leave a little tobacco.

I had kind of a funny experience coming back, talking to other archeologists; they all think highly of her. I said, "You have to stop talking about this archeologist as being an authority. I don't think she knows what's she's doing. To me, she's not looking at it the right way. She won't understand it." I could see that, so I closed the doors.

I went to a meeting of a rock art research group held in Green River. Before I left here, I read a newspaper article about a group of kids that went into Horse Canyon and actually took chalk and drew on the pictographs. The park service knew this group was going into that area. They trusted them. Eventually they took them to court, and the teenagers were fined so many thousand dollars. Their father had stood and watched them deface the pictographs yet he was an archeologist. Unbelievable.

So when I went there to speak, I said, "I want to read this article. We are not dealing with people who are just in the category of being totally ignorant about the Fremont period. We are talking about people who are supposed to be responsible. They are doing that, too, ruining everything." From there, I talked about the spirituality, how we look at it, what these markings mean to Indian people.

Afterward a lot of people came up and talked to me. There was a fellow who wrote a book on the meaning of rock art. He said, "You're the only one I've ever heard that had guts enough to tell an audience that these are spiritual things. Nobody's said that, but I believe that, too. You said what I wanted to say. They're spiritual things, not just writing on the wall."

I was telling them how I felt about it.

Then there was a lady who had done some videotaping down Desolation Canyon. They wanted to go down and take video and make a documentary about it, and put a spiritual element into it. The artists would be Indian artists, and they would contribute to the documentary. This woman is from Salt Lake City and works in a library in Salt Lake County. She had been here before. She got approval from the Business Council to proceed with her project, so she was going to look for grant money to put this together.

Her name came up in a meeting later on, and I said, "Well, I would like to express myself about this project. At this point, I feel skeptical. I don't like the idea. I would like to ask that she drop the whole thing." We asked the secretary to call and ask her to stop the project.

I said that for this reason: if we take these groups down, word will get out and other groups will be coming. Leave it alone. Just leave it alone. Don't tell anybody about it. If you publish it, you get a lot of people over there.

There were some panels in Book Cliffs, and a fellow who knew about them. He talked about taking pictures of them. A magazine tried to talk him into writing about all these areas. He was very reluctant but finally he decided to do two areas. So he described the two areas. Within three months, both places were vandalized—within three months! All the others were not. That's what I thought about, holding back information on certain places. With religion, it's the same way. We have to hold back things that have never been explored or other people will misuse them.

We have a lot of people who are Indian experts. We have a lot of expert Indians, too. But we have a lot of Indian experts that are not Indians.

The Return of the Uncompahgre

It never enters my mind to quit the Sun Dance or peyote meetings, or any spiritual ceremony. A sweat represents the darkness before the creation, also the womb; you are about to be reborn.

Long ago, there used to be a spirit to tell the future of any illness coming. It would say, "If you want to stay healthy, move away from here." It predicted the future. That spirit moved the Comanches from the Fort Bridger area to the plains and southward. The Utes moved to the east and south where it was warm.

One Sunday I was going to Colorado to a celebration, the one hundredth anniversary of the Grand Mesa National Forest. A scenic route association wants Indian dance groups to go down to Grand Junction and back into the Powder Horn ski resort. They have asked me to talk on history of the Uncompahgres, so that's why I went there.

For some time, I've been going to Steamboat Springs, Colorado, the center location of the Yampa or Whiteriver Utes. I go out with the archeologists into different areas, using their records, and visit these prehistoric sites. We find teepee rings (actually, they're not teepee rings, they're something else), and camp sites, and quarries where hunters would get materials to make arrowheads, and vision quest areas with trails.

Any situation always comes down to people again. The last few years, there have been people coming up from Ignacio, Colorado, and performing Indian dances through the Indian Affairs office in Denver. Since the Southern Utes live in Colorado, that office takes care of their people. When they need Indians, they go down to Ignacio or

Taowoc, and pick them up and they perform and talk about Indian ways. Then they have other tribes coming through there, and they do their sweat ceremonies. Also, they have these New Age people working with them, and the Indians charge them money to have a sweat. That happens a lot in that area.

Sometime later I was visiting with an archeologist in Montrose, and he brought up that same thing. These people come up to Montrose, Grand Junction, Ouray, and Gunnison, and they perform ceremonies. He wanted to know what I thought about that.

I said, "The first thing I would like to say is they are not what they call the Uncompahgre Utes. They are what we call the Mowach. They never were native to this area." They say they are the descendants of those people that lived there. Actually, a large group of Utes native to Colorado are now in Utah.

This was the first time they took a group from the Uintah-Ouray Reservation over there. We are actually the descendants of the Utes that lived there. I wanted to put full emphasis on that while I visited there—that we were bringing back the Uncompahgre.

But I'm not going to talk about us as Uncompahgres but us being Taviwatz—our true band name. Taviwatz came from a deeper part of the Rockies and the army moved them into the Uncompahgre River area; there, the Uncompahgre Agency was established.

Uncompahgre comes from two different names—they both could be right. There was a place there that had a pond up in the mountains, in a big flat area. The several ponds could make a small lake. The runoff coming from the mountains brought with it red dirt. So in clear water, you see the water being red—a red lake. The word Uncompahgre means red lake, and that's from those red ponds where the river flows down to the Colorado. That's where it comes from. Since it goes down into that valley, it became the Uncompahgre Valley; then the agency was called the Uncompahgre Agency, and eventually the Indians became called the Uncompahgres.

Also, when you go there and you look up, the hills are red because of a red oxide. Everywhere you look, it's red—an old mining area. The remnants of the old mining days are still there. So when you look at it you say, Uncompahgre Lake.

When I say these words to you, you don't know the difference. They sound the same to an outsider. Uncompahgre could mean Uncapahavit or Uncaparare. Uncompahgre could mean the lake or the hill, but they're both red. So that's how we got our name.

I am an Uncompahgre through my father. My father's mother, my grandmother, was an Uncompahgre. They lived there, then they moved over the state line to a place called the Book Cliff area where they had farms in the Bitter Creek area. We still have lots down there. That's where my grandmother lived, where my father was a young boy. My mother's people come from the upper area, the Yampahtika. So when I was enrolled in the tribal record, I was enrolled on my mother's side, as a Yampa Ute—the carrot eaters, they were called. However, when the people held the agency at Meeker on the White River, they changed the name to the Whiteriver Agency, so that's where the band name comes from. When the army brought them to this reservation in Utah, along with them came the new names: the Whiteriver Utes and the Uncompahgre Utes. But they're both wrong. They're the Yampahtika and the Taviwatz. That's how that came about.

My grandfather on my father's side was Uintah—John Duncan was a Uintah. Actually, I think he was part of what they call a Timpknuwech, which was a Ute word meaning the one that lives near a rocky mountain. Those people were up in Logan, the Heber Valley, and back toward Evanston and Fort Bridger, Wyoming. They were somewhat tied in with the sheep eaters, a mixed group living close together. They spoke Shoshone, and they spoke Ute. The Bannocks are similar, in between Ute and Shoshone. The dialects are different. That's why they call it Kumabahpagi.

My talk was based on how the groups were actually called. When they call on people to come and do certain things, we would like to be

the ones they notify first. Then if we don't want to do it, they can call
the other ones. We're not separating; we're not going to say we're a
different people. They're merely a group that came from another area.
If we are going to present something on the history of the Utes, let's
do it right.

Indian Way and the World

This morning I was singing some peyote songs, and I was telling my family, "I'm thinking about going to Kiowa country. I know they're having a hard time. They're losing their old people. An old man, one of the elders, is sick. I would like to be there with him, say something. When I was a young boy, I was adopted into the peyote ceremonies of a Kiowa family, along with my mother, a father, brothers, sisters, aunts, uncles. It was done in this ceremony. The teepee was put up just for that one purpose, to adopt us. I want to go back and contribute something, maybe pray for them, think about them.

Once in Oklahoma, in Kiowa country, I went to a peyote meeting. It was winter and very cold. During the meeting, I began wondering about how things were at home. I closed my eyes and felt myself lifted up. Then I was walking around my house, from room to room. Everything was still. My family was sleeping. Then I was lifted back somehow and opened my eyes. I was in the meeting again.

The Kiowas have a spiritual power that's theirs, but they've made it too easy for outsiders. They are too lax in the way they treat people. The Navajos go there, and they learn the Kiowa ways, then go back. But the Navajos don't do ceremonies the way the Kiowas do; with the Navajos, it's like a big show. I've seen that happen. When the Kiowas let their ways go and gave it to other people, they knew that they shouldn't have done that. My father said, "When this peyote gets into trouble, it's going to be not here among the Utes, but from the tribe down that way. They're too open. They're the ones that are going to get into trouble." That's what he said.

Then I've got part of the Kiowa way here; it's become part of my way. I sing Kiowa songs because of my relationship with the tribe. People may think I sing in Kiowa just for show, but it's not that. I was adopted into the Kiowas. I also use our songs, or songs I learned from Comanches. I mix them. In the morning time I use Kiowa songs. Their words talk about sunrise, getting close to God, or light—ways of being in the world.

These songs may be an entry for me to understand what is actually taking place. I found myself talking about the Kiowa doll. The Kiowas, a long time ago, lost a doll, the image of a man in full regalia. When they had the Sun Dance, they'd tie that doll on to the pole. They lost the doll—they had a couple of them. The Utes got that doll. The Kiowas lose their ways. Eventually, they might get the doll back.

I will go back to them and tell them I will pray that they will get the doll back, get it away from the people that took it. God's spirit is going to do that. Then it will be all right.

The Utes have the Sun Dance now. The Comanches and the Kiowas are brother tribes. The Kiowas taught the Comanches how to Sun Dance. A Comanche fellow went back up into the Wyoming area and brought the Sun Dance to his Shoshone brothers. A man from here went to the Shoshones and brought the Sun Dance here. The Sun Dance we have is a Kiowa Sun Dance. So is peyote.

Recently I set up my white teepee. I was waiting for my nephew, but he didn't show up. I asked some guests, non-Indians, to help me. As we worked, I explained to them what the teepee means to me.

The world is round, the teepee is round. You have different denominations in this world, but they all go to one place and they are all tied together. The ropes come down from different points. Next I will throw the canvas on. The canvas is a cover, and that's our universe. It opens for smoke to go out around the world, in the spiritual way. The door is always to the east. You always go to the south and around. All things that you do travel around.

My religion is like going into a teepee. A teepee sits in a circle. It only has one door, and that's in the east where the sun comes up. As the sun goes around, there's darkness in the teepee, too. When you're born into this world, light comes from the east; the whole circle is your life. When your life ends, it goes back out that way again.

Sometimes we have peyote meetings every week. Sometimes every other week; sometimes we don't go to a meeting for a month. If it's available, if people are having meetings, then we go. It depends on the families. I would sponsor a meeting, a religious meeting; then the next family might sponsor one the following week; it moves around. The hosts select their own chiefs, and from there things are all the same, yet each meeting is different. They conduct their services basically all the same. The way that it is handled is a little different. You will never see exactly the same thing twice at a spiritual meeting. So that means sometimes I can go to a meeting four or five times in a month.

Once in a great while, only in a time of need, have I ever experienced a meeting four nights in a row. There was a person who was sick. He had somehow lost part of his mind; it wasn't all there. His relations said, "Well, let's have a peyote meeting and pray that he will get his mind back." He would be all right for a little while, and then all at once he would slip into this other thing again. He would start hitting things; they would have to grab things away from him and hold him down.

We had different people run meetings. During the day we watched him, kept really close watch over him. On the fourth night, we moved from one place to another place. The fourth night was east of White Rocks. I was there. I was sitting by him. My brother was sitting on the other side. We started off the same way.

About midnight or around there, he said, "I would like to sleep for a while. I'm tired."

We said, "Go ahead." You know, he really slept soundly, right there, sitting up between us while the meeting was going on. Then toward morning he woke up. The chief put cedar on the charcoal, and the staff was coming around the circle. It was his turn to sing. Feathers, sage…he was on his knees; he would sing four songs. He started off kind of weakly. You could tell he was getting off balance. The second song was a little stronger. The third one was better than the first two. And with the fourth song, he seemed to open up. Then he passed the staff on, and said, "I want to say something."

He said, "I don't know where I've been, or what's going on. I know that I've been sick. I'm all right."

The chief put cedar on to sanctify his words, and that was it. We had a meeting four nights in a row. He's been all right ever since.

Four nights in a row—you're not sleeping. When you're helping a sick person, you're thinking about that person alone. My brothers were there, too. We were all contributing to this. One would be with him, then another.

Nowadays, we don't have too many meetings. In the summertime, peyote slacks off. There are more powwows. In the fall, we'll be going back to meetings again.

I'm having a meeting at my house. There's an Arapahoe family from Wyoming; the wife is from here. Several years ago, they made a vow that they'd hold a meeting. So they figure that things have been going wrong in their lives; so they want to fulfill that vow. They wanted me to go to Wyoming, but I told them no. I'll have the meeting here. I'm making contact with different ones that should be there. So that's the next meeting. But this week, I'll be in Colorado, then I'm coming back and going to Phoenix, then back to Salt Lake again for the Indian tribes meeting. After that, I'm going to the national meeting.

The Southern Utes and Ute Mountain Utes have their own spiritual leaders. The title I hold, president of the Native American Church of Utah, has a meaning to both the American and Native American sides. On the reservation, I chair the business meetings and take care of the paperwork—such as renewing the charter with the state. When there is a big conference of all the tribal leaders, Native American Church leaders, I go there. Then I come back and report. Or if there's any paperwork to be done with the state of Texas, where the peyote's grown, then I would take care of that. So they look at me as a business leader.

Of course, I run meetings, too; that's a different way of looking at it. We are not designated by the whole as leaders, only by those who ask you to do certain things. They know that you are merely conducting that meeting as a spiritual leader for the spirit itself.

When people talk about Southern Utes and the Native American Church, that is not in my jurisdiction. I have nothing to do with the Goshutes, Paiutes, and no authority over those other groups except that I go to meetings with them.

Recently I was asked by people to respond to an activity, which was rather negative. The Southern Utes had a split. One group was actually inviting non-Indians to peyote meetings. By federal law, that's wrong. Non-Indians are not supposed to use peyote. But they invited them. There has been some write-up in the drug magazines about this. A writer from New York came, took pictures, and published the article in a drug magazine. Other Southern Utes broke away from them; they say that twice this has happened. In one family, after they'd been working with hippies, a couple of them actually divorced their wives and married two of the hippie women.

In addition to all this, they are making money through letting outsiders into the ceremony. The complaint I heard is this: the magazine, this last time, paid them eight hundred dollars. What they gave them before is not known, but it was a large amount of money. They accepted that money.

So the group that split away came up here and said they would like me to intervene. They wanted to have a peyote meeting so I could go down and tell them that their group would be aligned with us. The other part will be cut away. I said, "Well, you could do it by yourselves." But they've been having problems, particularly at Ignacio.

Around June, I went down there, joining the chairman of the Native American Church of Oklahoma. I took care of the fire. I was somewhat uncomfortable with the situation. I like to keep my hands clean, wash them off. There's a dark side to this. The dark side is people, how people use spiritual power, what they do with it. A lot of questions have to be answered. The destruction of these ceremonies is going to come from within. This group is leading toward that.

Also the leaders of those ceremonies, who were accepting money from white people, are actually self-appointed—but they are looked at as medicine people. They have tricks that they learn, magic tricks. They have different beliefs. Then they say it's an Indian belief—witching each other, or somebody witching. They'll all go against them in a spiritual way, so they will die. Those kind of things come in. The southern groups are strong on witching because the Navajos are that way: they believe in witching. Most Navajo ceremonies involve cleansing the witching because that's what makes them sick. So they have the ceremonies to heal that. Here, we don't have that.

My mother is very old and frail. Last night I had a dream. In my dream, I saw a man who is gone now, but who once gave my mother some feathers; I think she still has them. He was moving around, performing a ceremony, and behind him came a young boy pulling a red cloth.

I've been thinking about that all morning. When I get back to the Basin, I'm going to ask my mother about those feathers. I want to fulfill that dream.

One night I dreamed I had ended my life and gone into the next world. I saw before me an enormous man, an Indian man sitting cross-legged, wearing a breechcloth. He was so big, I could only see his feet, his legs, and his torso. He asked me about my life.

I answered his questions, but I didn't answer all of them quite right. He said, "Why are you lying to me? I know you did things this way, not that other way."

I thought, *Who is this? How does he know when I'm lying?*

I took another step back so I could see his face. This enormous man—this Indian questioning me—was myself.

30

The Olympics

Eleven years ago, the Indian tribes were invited to participate in the 2002 Winter Olympics ceremony.[1] The Games were being held in Salt Lake City and the Indians were chosen to carry the flame; only a few people were selected for that. It all began when the Olympic Committee notified the tribal offices.

My tribal office got a call from Salt Lake and a man said, "I want to talk to Clifford Duncan." I got on the phone and he asked me, "Do you want to carry the torch for the Olympics? You're going to need a passport."

I said, "All right. I can do that." It was during that time that I went to Athens, Greece.

On the way there, security was really tight because it was right after 9/11. We'd get on a bus and they'd check all of us and look at our visas and passports. Then, they'd transport us in a bus across their grounds and then they'd check us again when we got off. We'd go into the gate and they'd check us once again. That took a lot of time, but it was a part of the experience, I guess.

We arrived in Greece on a big airplane that was thirteen seats across. We didn't stop anywhere; it was a direct flight from Salt Lake City to Athens. They got each of us a room when we got there, but I never went to bed because I was so busy. I didn't have time to travel anywhere either, I just stayed close to the hotel.

---

1 Carolyn Janecek interviewed Clifford Duncan in 2013, years after Linda Sillitoe's death, and composed this chapter from the interview.

We went to that old Colosseum for the passing of the torch. Mitt Romney had come with us; he was in charge of the Olympic organizing committee. The torch was handed to him and then he gave it to each one of us, letting us hold it. That's all that really happened.

I liked Athens; it was a beautiful town, right at the edge of the land and water at once. I liked being able to see the ocean. It was a good experience.

Coming back, we stopped in Atlanta, Georgia. From there, the torch went across the country, while we returned to Utah by plane. In Salt Lake, they put us up at the Little America, a real fancy hotel with big marble fireplaces in the lobby and an expensive restaurant. They were good to us.

During that time, we had to do a lot of rehearsals, where they told us how it was going to be. It wasn't very exciting.

Five tribes were supposed to take part in the ceremony: the Ute, Paiute, Navajo, Shoshone, and Goshute. A lead man would ride a horse: five horses and five tribes, coming in from different entrances. Each rider would lead a small procession through his entrance, following him were the dancers from his tribe, who came on foot, all dressed up. The Utes came in from the south.

In the center, the singers and drummers were on a stage that moved around on the ice, providing music for the dancers. A drum group rode around and slid over the ice while drumming away. At the top, someone played the flute. That was kind of interesting.

I was one of the leaders, so they put me on a horse. It was very cold and the ground was icy; I had to ride the horse along a sort of boardwalk and then walk him onto the ice. I thought I was going to slide all over, but the horse was pretty steady. When each of the riders got to a certain place, we were supposed to get off.

One night, we were having a rehearsal. There was this Paiute lady riding with us; she was kind of heavy set and short. Anyway, we got to our places on the ice and each one of us got off: first, second, third, fourth. It was the Paiute lady's turn, and she got off all right, but she disappeared. Her moccasins slid on the ice and she went under the horse. She was screaming as she lay there. That was funny.

But then I started thinking, 'Well, if she fell, then I'm so old that I'm going to fall too.' So I was real careful getting off....I made it.

At that time, a large group of people was supposed to be there, who didn't come. The Southern Utes from Ignacio were afraid of the risks after the 9/11 terrorist attacks, so they just pulled out.

I was talking to my aunt about this. I said, "You know them Southern Utes, they canceled. They were afraid a big bomb could go off, killing all of those people at the Olympics."

"Look at it this way," she says. "If you happen to die while you're there, at least you'll be dying with a big bang." That was fun.

After that, they told me to talk to the athletes. When all of the athletes were lined up in front of me, they said, "You talk."

I said, "All right." And I spoke to all of them in Ute.

Finally, this Goshute boy, Rupert Steele, asked me, "Clifford, what did you say to them athletes? All those athletes were from another country; they don't understand you. What did you tell them?"

I teased him, "I told them to pack up their stuff and go home; that's what I said, 'Get out of here,' and all them athletes were happy."

He laughed.

The Indians had a big part in the Olympics that year. I think that was good. Utah was named after the Utes, but we don't get a lot of recognition.

We call people who are not Indians *marikahns*, because when the white people first met the Indians, they pointed at themselves, saying, "Americans. You're an Indian. I'm American."

The Utes, instead of saying "Americans," said, *marikahns*; they were trying to say "American." *Marikahns* became a word for *them*, not *us*.

Today, when we are watching the TV and the president says, "God bless America," the Indians will say, "He's not talking about Indians, he's talking about him, because that's what they call each other: *mari-kahns*, Americans." He didn't say "people" and that's where we're separated.

Long ago, that white man said he was *marihkahns* and that we were not. The meaning behind that didn't change; cultural differences are imbedded into language and each side hears what is being said differently.

With the Olympics, America really recognized the Indians for the first time. There hasn't been anything like that since.

31

The Hospital

Everything seems kind of like a memory.[1] If I go somewhere, I can remember where that was. My daughter stays with me now that my eyesight is so bad; she drives for me too. When she goes downtown with the grandkids, I can give her directions from memory. I tell her, "Over there, you're going to get to this. Then, when you get to that, turn left." I can't see the top of the mountains anymore.

I got away from Indian dancing because it's totally different than how it used to be. Last Fourth of July I went down. I dressed up in my Indian outfit and went down for one evening for the big celebration. I felt like a baby learning how to walk, just stumbling around.

I remember going to the hospital last night. People came over to the house, saying, "We're going to take you to the hospital."

I said, "No, let me sleep for a while. Go wait outside or something."

I've got a room here at the hospital now. I'll be staying here a couple of days, relaxing until they send me home.

The doctor said my kidneys are shot. I don't feel any pain, I just feel sick. Sometimes, I think I might not even be sick. It's just in the way a person feels. You think it, but you're not really sick, only a part of you is sick. When something breaks, you just fix that specific part, like in a car or a computer; I want to hit the right button and get better.

I told my children to sprinkle some tobacco into the fire at home, to help me. When you make a fire and put tobacco in it, you're lighting

---

1   Carolyn Janecek interviewed Clifford Duncan in 2013, years after Linda Sillitoe's death, and composed this chapter from the interview.

a fire to your prayers. You give that tobacco to the fire and ask the fire
to pray for you, but the fire won't tell you anything; ceremonies will
only give you a glimpse of the truth. You have to look for it; it's hard,
and you can't ever say that something is certain or clear. Nothing is
ever truly exposed, because we, people, have only ever scratched the
surface of the Earth.

I'll be all right.

Men's Northern Traditional eagle feather dance bustle. Clifford made this for himself and danced with it in his younger days. Photographed at Clifford Duncan's home in Neola, Utah.

NOVEMBER 25, 2016.